Loss of a Baby

Understanding Maternal Grief

Loss of a Baby

---- ❧ ----

DEATH OF A DREAM

MARGARET NICOL

■ HarperCollins*Publishers*

HarperCollins*Publishers*

First published in Australia in 1989 by Bantam Books
This edition 1997 by HarperCollins*Publishers* Pty Limited
ACN 009 913 517
A member of the HarperCollins*Publishers* (Australia) Pty Limited Group

Copyright © Iris Diamond 1997, 1989

HarperCollins*Publishers*
25 Ryde Road, Pymble, Sydney NSW 2073, Australia
31 View Road, Glenfield, Auckland 10, New Zealand
77–85 Fulham Palace Road, London W6 8JB, United Kingdom
Hazelton Lanes, 55 Avenue Road, Suite 2900, Toronto, Ontario, M5R 3L2
and 1995 Markham Road, Scarborough, Ontario M1B 5M8, Canada
10 East 53rd Street, New York NY 10032, USA

The National Library of Australia Cataloguing-in-Publication data:

Nicol, Margaret.
    Loss of a baby : understanding maternal grief.
    {New ed.}.
    ISBN 0 7322 5869 3.
    1. Grief. 2. Bereavement – Psychological aspects. 3.
    Infants – Death – Psychological aspects. 4. Infants
    (Newborn) – Death – Psychological aspects. 5. Parent and
    child. I. Title.
155.937

'Pieta' by James McAuley, from his *Collected Poems*, 1994, is reprinted by permission of
HarperCollins*Publishers*.
'Love—Gratitude by Elisabeth Kübler-Ross is from *Death: the final stage of growth*,
Prentice-Hall.
Poems by Ainslie Meares are from *A kind of believing*, Hill of Content, Melbourne.
Reprinted with permission.

Printed in Australia by Griffin Press, Adelaide
9 8 7 6 5 4 3 2 1
99 98 97

Acknowledgements

This book is dedicated to all the mothers and fathers who have grieved over the loss of a baby and to the memory of those children.

My gratitude goes to Dr. Jeff Tompkins, Professor Pat Giles and Brian Heath; not only for their significant chapters, but for their ongoing support, encouragement and friendship. I would like to acknowledge also the memory of Professor Robin Winkler, who believed in and supported this work.

My understanding and appreciation of the uniqueness of the inner journey has been deeply enriched by Professor Russell Meares. I owe a great deal as well to the writings of the late Dr. Ainslie Meares.

Most importantly I wish to acknowledge my son David. His presence in my life has given me more than words can express and taught me the true depth and beauty of the bond.

THE WATER-LILY

A lonely young Wife
In her dreaming discerns
A lily-decked pool
With a border of ferns,
And a beautiful child,
With butterfly wings,
Trips down to the edge of the water and sings:
    'Come, mamma! come!
    'Quick! follow me—
'Step out on the leaves of the water-lily!'

And the lonely young wife,
Her heart beating wild,
Cries, 'Wait till I come,
'Till I reach you, my child!'
But the beautiful child
With the butterfly wings
Steps out on the leaves of the lily and sings:
    'Come, mamma! come!
    'Quick! follow me!
'And step on the leaves of the water-lily!'

And the wife in her dreaming
Steps out on the stream,
But the lily leaves sink
And she wakes from her dream.
Ah, the waking is sad,
For the tears that it brings
And she knows 'tis her dead baby's spirit that sings:
    'Come, mamma! come!
    'Quick! follow me!
'Step out on the leaves of the water-lily!'

Henry Lawson

Contents

Foreword

I have come to know Margaret Nicol as a sensitive and compassionate therapist. Her book reflects these qualities.

The book concerns a relatively neglected part of the catalogue of human loss. It focusses particularly on losses which many people in a woman's environment do not respond to as if they were significant or painful events. Examples of such events include miscarriage, abortion, infertility and stillbirth. The consequence for the woman is a sense of isolation, alienation and loneliness which may reverberate through the family undermining major relationships, as the stories in the book illustrate.

The book also addresses the effect of losses which are more clearly seen for what they are. They include neonatal death, cot death, the birth of a handicapped child and adoption. Nevertheless, those around the woman may not acknowledge her grief, perhaps because of the difficulty of the subject and because, in our society, grief is still one of the things about which we often do not speak. Margaret Nicol, in a study of women in such a situation, showed that they suffer a very considerable amount of physical and mental ill-health. This may have been avoided had those around them responded so as to give reality to the feelings a woman may have tried to hide, including sometimes feelings of guilt. The author points out that one does not need to be an expert to help in such a situation. A sensitive capacity to listen may be all that is needed.

A particularly valuable and moving aspect of the book is the large number of verbatim reports from women who have lost babies in various ways. Their stories will be helpful to the large number of people who experience a loss and feel cut-off from others since they feel their responses are unusual or will not be understood. These people will include not only the women themselves, but also husbands and other family members. Margaret Nicol makes clear that the losses she describes are so common as to be a likely event in most women's lives. In this sense, it is a book about every woman.

The author writes about her subject in a way which allows it to be understood in its imaginative context. She shows that the mother's feelings about, and her preoccupation in, her child often begin well before birth and that the loss of those fantasies shakes the mother in a way which may not be grasped by those around her.

This book should help not only those who have lost a baby but also those professionals who encounter the bereaved in their working lives.

Professor Russell Meares

Introduction

The love that links a woman to her baby is the deepest of human bonds. Thus, the most devastating experience a woman can suffer is the breaking of that bond through the death or loss of her baby. When that loss comes at a time which is normally joyful, the pain is almost incomprehensible. Reality is shattered. Yet it is not just the mother's sense of reality of the loss of her baby that is destroyed, but her whole maternal experience. It becomes shrouded in silence. Such an overwhelming trauma for the mother is often treated as a nonevent, because our society considers this to be an unspeakable subject. Close friends and relatives may not even mention that the baby existed, let alone mention the loss. Why is there such a conspiracy of silence?

Initially the focus of this book was based on my research on maternal grief following stillbirth or neonatal death. However, the more I have talked with women and come to understand the impact of reproductive losses, the clearer it has become that this grief is not merely the experience of a minority of women. The book has evolved to include all major losses; incorporating miscarriage, cot death, the birth of a handicapped child, infertility, adoption and termination. In viewing the whole spectrum of reproductive losses, it felt to me that this must be an experience shared by many women in our community. Yet, I could find no substantiation for this feeling and the enormity of the subject seemed to be subverted by the silence pervading it.

As this book came to completion, I spoke of this issue to Dr. Fiona Stanley and Dr. Anne Read of the Department of

Epidemiology at the University of Western Australia. Subsequently, they analysed Western Australian statistics on reproductive losses for the years 1984–86. The results of these analyses were quite staggering. From their findings we can extrapolate that of all women in Australia of reproductive age (i.e. between fourteen and forty-four years of age), ten per cent suffer some form of reproductive loss each year. It is estimated that on average, every woman would suffer approximately three reproductive losses by the age of forty-four. This figure is particularly thought-provoking if one considers that by the time a woman is nearing the end of her own reproductive life, she is then likely to become a grandmother and experience the grief and trauma associated with the reproductive losses of her daughters and/or daughters-in-law. These loss rates can be extended to other members of the woman's family such as her sisters, and her friends. Therefore the grief that impinges on women's lives in relation to reproductive loss is indeed considerable. Women often suffer a lonely, isolated grief, each tending to believe that she is the only one who feels the way she does.

The intense emotional pain and isolation that women suffer was clearly conveyed to me in my research on maternal grief when I interviewed one hundred and ten women who had experienced either a stillbirth or neonatal death. Over the past twenty-five years, while the perinatal (stillbirths and neonatal deaths) mortality rate in Australia has declined by more than half, the needs of these bereaved women are increasing. Because the perinatal death rate has lessened, women are less likely to be prepared for it and there are fewer people around to turn to for support, who have themselves suffered a similar loss and who can understand.

Prior to 1970, there had been no studies on the effects of a stillbirth or neonatal death on the mother's physical and mental health. No information on the need to support the bereaved mother could be found in any medical textbook or journal. The first major study in this area was conducted by Professor Pat Giles at King Edward Memorial Hospital for Women in Perth. During the 1970's an increased awareness had developed that the death of a baby can have a major impact on the health and well-being of women and their families.

Changes had been made in some hospitals and in the support available to bereaved mothers in the community. Yet there remained many unanswered questions, which I felt needed to be answered by the bereaved mothers themselves, in order for them to ultimately receive the support they needed.

In 1980 Dr. Jeff Tompkins and I began our research into maternal grieving following perinatal death. The foundation of my initial research evolved from the experiences conveyed to me by the women members of the Stillbirth And Neonatal Death Support group (SANDS), a group which had been established for bereaved parents in Perth. A survey of the medical literature in this area suggested to me that the pattern of grief reactions was thought to be similar to the classical descriptions of grief after the death of an adult loved one. However, there had been no research done which assessed the physical and psychological effects on women in order to determine the degree and extent of their loss. In talking with SANDS members, it emerged that although their grief was very real and very intense, it was not acknowledged by those around them.

A crucial aspect of my research, then, was to investigate the reality of this maternal grief, which was described by the women in SANDS. It was important not only to investigate the depth of women's reactions, but to try to determine what assisted women to a healthy resolution of grief and what predisposed them to an unresolved grief. I wanted to find out from bereaved mothers what their needs were and what they found to be helpful and unhelpful experiences. If health care professionals and the community could understand more deeply the experiences and needs of bereaved mothers, then changes could be made to assist these women to a healthy grief resolution.

One hundred and ten women contributed to this study. Each woman was asked specific questions and each told a unique story of the loss of her baby and her own journey through grief. When the information and ideas from all the women were combined, it was clearly a very powerful statement of both their experiences and needs.

Shortly after the research results were published in a local newspaper, I received a telephone call from a woman who had lost her first and only baby twenty-five years ago. It is a call I shall always remember. She explained that after the death of her son, she returned to her home in the country. She had not seen her son or had a funeral. In fact, she had nothing to indicate he had ever existed. When she went home, her husband never mentioned the birth or the death. No family member or anyone in her community said a word, there was only silence. The pain she bore she did so on her own, and she said that it was the worst pain she had ever experienced. She decided not to have any more children because she felt she just could not tolerate the prospect of going through it again.

She talked to me for over two hours of all the vivid memories of her dreams for this son, and the grief of so many years. I was riveted by the intensity of her words ... 'For twenty-five years I have not spoken to anyone about my son, or what I went through. I am ringing you today to say I hope through work such as yours women will not have to go through it alone.' Through listening to her I really understood the tyranny of silence in our society. It was then I decided to write a book for bereaved mothers, but it was to take six years, as there was still much I needed to learn and understand.

In 1982, I was awarded the Women's Fellowship by the Western Australian Government for my work with bereaved mothers in our community. This gave me the opportunity to travel to England, Canada and the United States to study innovations in services for bereaved parents. Visits to a variety of hospitals and community support groups, and discussions with health care workers and bereaved parents were invaluable in broadening my knowledge. I also gained practical ideas and guidelines as to the most effective forms of health care services within hospitals and the community.

Over the past six years I have seen many bereaved women bringing the full range of reproductive losses to my awareness. Through them I have learned that one can never classify or quantify grief. The depth of grief experienced by women regardless of the type of loss is uniquely their own private journey. Working with these women, who are dealing with their loss and ultimately their own healing process, has deepened and enriched my perspective and has been essential to my understanding.

When I began writing this book, I felt it was important to include the personal stories of bereaved women. To this end, I asked women I had the privilege of working with through research, SANDS or within therapy, to write of their own experiences. These stories are interwoven throughout the book. Although selected to highlight a particular theme of a chapter, the stories all have aspects relevant to every other chapter. Initially I felt I would comment on each story, but as I received and read each one individually I realised they were self-contained and needed neither enhancement nor elucidation. They were complete within themselves, for they are spoken from the heart.

This book, in a very real sense, is written by hundreds of women who have so openly conveyed the inner experience of their grief. It is written to help newly bereaved parents with the hope that out of the isolation and loneliness can come communication, understanding and support. This book is about breaking the silence.

Chapter 1

Maternal grief:
the breaking
of the bond

LOVE—Gratitude

The agony is so great . . .
And yet I will stand it.
Had I not loved so very much
I would not hurt so much.
But goodness knows I would not
Want to diminish that precious love
By one fraction of an ounce.
I will hurt.
And I will be grateful to the hurt
For it bears witness to
The depth of our meanings,
And for that I will be
Eternally grateful.

Elisabeth Kübler-Ross

'When my baby died, it felt like a part of me died too.'

This statement expresses the feelings of many women who have suffered the loss of their baby. How can the death of a baby a woman may never have seen affect her so profoundly?

Women come to see me sometimes only to get reassurance that they are not crazy, because the real experiences of their bereavement are not reflected in their support group or by our society. When such an extreme mismatch occurs between a person's inner experience and what is happening in the world around them, the conflict must be resolved. Unfortunately, women tend to assume that the fault lies within themselves—for how could all those people out there be wrong? When women talk in their confusion and despair, I explain that to resolve grief after the loss of a baby is like trying to be sane in an insane world. I have never met a bereaved mother whose feelings were not real, appropriate and valid for her. The craziness is in the mismatch of the reaction of those who do not understand.

One key to understanding maternal grief is to understand the bond between mother and infant. While it is often assumed that this bond begins at birth, it actually develops and deepens throughout the pregnancy. In some cases, the relationship may begin even before conception.

In our society today, many families decide to have a specific number of children, often just two, and these are usually planned in advance. In these circumstances, women begin thinking of or imagining the children they hope to have, well before the pregnancy. Much preparation is made by the couple to ensure that they have what they feel is necessary to begin their family. Intertwined with the planning are the woman's hopes and dreams for her unborn child. In this way a woman subtly begins to form an attachment to her future children and when the pregnancy is confirmed, her dreams are made real. A woman may not even be consciously aware of how much a part of her life this future child has become. It is quite obvious when one listens to pregnant women in conversation: there may be talk of what sex the baby will be; names will be chosen and rechosen; ideas of who the baby may look like or how it will fit in the family are discussed; hopes for the baby's future will emerge and the mother becomes preoccupied with her baby.

Although there are always fears or concerns regarding the pregnancy, the mother develops a trust that her baby will be born alive, normal and healthy. As the pregnancy progresses, there is often dialogue between the mother and her baby. Her physical and emotional relationship with the baby is real and deep. The months of pregnancy have formed the basis for that strongest, most intimate bond, between mother and infant. When this bond is broken through the death of the baby, the devastation reverberates throughout the mother, for they have been together as one. Her trust in life has been shattered and a very real part of her has died.

The loss experienced by a woman following the death of her baby is extremely complex as it involves facing multiple losses. The mother grieves for the loss of her baby as a special person. She also grieves for the loss of the baby that was a part of her. Normally, after a woman gives birth she will feel a sense of emptiness which is related to the loss by birth of the baby inside her. This transitional experience is usually reconciled within a few weeks as the relationship with her newborn baby develops. However, when death and birth occur in a parallel process, the mother feels both losses—her baby whom she can see and hold and also her fullness of pregnancy with her inner infant.

Alongside these losses is the loss of all her hopes and dreams for her child. To others, this baby may be only an unknown child. To the mother, her baby is deeply known and loved. The mother has many links to the baby's past and through to the future. She often intuitively knows her baby well, through all the memories and daydreams she has of her child. Thus she will need to mourn not only her child, but the whole person that child might have been.

Another area of loss to be dealt with is related to the woman's perception of herself as a partner to her husband, and as a mother. Usually when a woman decides to become pregnant, she has a positive view of herself as wife/partner, who will be a good mother to a happy, healthy baby. When the baby dies, a woman's self-esteem can be shaken a great deal. Her sense of womanhood, femininity, sexuality and strength may all come into question.

Intermingled with all these losses a woman will experience the full gamut of her emotions. Her feelings initially can range from anger, rage, bitterness, sadness, through to shame, guilt, loneliness and despair. She can also vary from feeling nothing to a sense of being like an emotional volcano. No experience she has had can prepare her for the anguish she feels after the loss of her baby.

The paradox is that the outside world so often denies a bereaved mother her sense of reality. A lack of understanding by family and friends, or health care professionals, of the depth of the mother's bond with her baby and the extent of her many losses, can compound the mother's distress. So many women say that they receive well-meaning comments suggesting 'It was only a baby you never knew—just get pregnant again.' There is also a sense that if they cry or mention the birth or death, a hushed silence overcomes the conversation and the topic is changed.

People believe that they will save the mother from pain if they never allow the baby to be mentioned. The effect of this misconception is to block her grief from its healthy natural course. Eventually bereaved mothers no longer speak their thoughts or express their feelings because it upsets those whom they love. This seeming lack of compassion forces the bereaved mother to care more for the feelings of those around her than for her own needs and she retreats to isolation to relive her memories of her child, and to try to soothe herself.

The myths that surround maternal grief need to be challenged in our community. Bereaved mothers need to receive the acknowledgement that their baby existed and was loved and special. They need their family and friends to understand that their loss and their grief is real.

Deafening silence

Each baby's birth has been special to me and carries loving memories, but of my six children, I remember the events surrounding the birth of Jane, much clearer and in more detail.

She was the third child, after her brother and sister had been born healthy, with trouble-free pregnancies. So it was with confidence I announced to our little children that they would be having a little brother or sister, and they were prepared to greet her into the family.

The pregnancy was not an easy one, as I didn't feel too well throughout most of the nine months and three weeks before our daughter was born. I went into labour and went to hospital and then everything stopped. So, I was a little unsettled by the time I eventually got going the second time. Even though I was uneasy, I was not prepared for what happened.

When our daughter was born there was absolute silence. The silence was deafening and frightening, something I will never forget. Then, after what seemed like hours, but could have been only seconds, I heard a tiny cry. My heart lifted and I thought 'Everything is fine', but still more silence. Finally, the doctor spoke, 'There is something wrong with your little girl, but I am not sure what'. I couldn't believe it— 'Something wrong with my baby—not me—I'm normal, I don't have something wrong with my babies.' Then the sister came up . . . 'What are you calling your baby, dear?' She wanted to baptise her. There really was something wrong.

My doctor was superb. Right from the beginning he spoke honestly and tried to inform me of everything he knew. He even offered to go to our home and babysit the other children, while my husband came to the hospital. At 3 a.m. in the morning! Finally, my bewildered husband arrived and we cried together, but mostly we were too shocked to realise what was happening.

In the eighteen hours Jane lived, we missed out on so much of her life. I only saw her once after she left the labour ward and that was through the glass of the nursery on my way to my room. Sometimes, twenty-three years later, I try to picture in my mind what she looked like, how she lay, if she had any hair; but in my mind there is only an imaginary little baby girl, perfect in every way. There were many times in those eighteen hours when I believed I was dreaming, or thought someone would come in and say there had been a mistake—she wasn't sick after all—so I guess I never gave up hope till she finally died.

Coming home to two pre-schoolers, who were expecting a little baby to come with me, was very hard, and the first few weeks at home I spent telling them, time and time again, that our baby was sick, and had died and was now in heaven. Our 2½-year-old daughter would ask visitors to the house to come and see baby's clothes and show them all the room prepared for her.

Friends and relatives generally were kind and helpful but I always felt they didn't really understand our loss. My main aim was to get pregnant again as quickly as possible, which I did. Eleven months later after a mentally traumatic pregnancy, our son was born healthy and strong. I went on to have another daughter and son, but never again did I take for granted that a healthy baby would be born.

Jane is still very much part of our family. Even the three children born after her, consider her as their sister. When our youngest was in primary school they had to write in class about their family, and he included our lost daughter. The teacher came to me and in hushed tones told me what my son had done. Much to her amazement I said how delighted I was, which left her thinking we were both a little 'strange'.

Since becoming grandparents, babies have become even more precious to us, and my husband recently remarked that it is only now that he really appreciates the significance to us of losing our little daughter. However, she is and always will be a member of our family; our third child, a precious memory, our special angel, and the sadness and pain of her birth and death somehow has added meaning to our lives.

Chapter 2

Women's reactions to the death of a baby

PIETÀ

A year ago you came
Early into the light.
You lived a day and night,
Then died; no one to blame.

Once only, with one hand,
Your mother in farewell
Touched you. I cannot tell,
I cannot understand

A thing so dark and deep,
So physical a loss:
One touch, and that was all

She had of you to keep.
Clean wounds, but terrible,
Are those made with the Cross.

James McAuley

In order to understand the reality of women's experiences following the death of their babies, an investigation was conducted into the nature and incidence of psychological effects in mothers who had experienced a perinatal death. Each woman was personally interviewed using the Mother-

Infant Questionnaire developed for this study (Nicol, 1980). The questionnaire was adapted from a general health questionnaire used to assess changes in the health of women following the death of a husband (Madison & Walker, 1967). It included an assessment of the women's present and past life factors, their experiences in hospital, their perception of the support they received, and an assessment of their health.

The women in the study had experienced either a stillbirth or neonatal death in the three years prior to the interview. They lived within the Perth metropolitan area or were prepared to visit Perth for the interview. There was a wide range of hospitals in which their babies had been born, so the hospital experiences differed greatly. The women were aged from nineteen to forty-one years. The majority were married or in a de facto relationship. Most were Australian-born.

In order to assess the effects of the loss of their baby on their health, the women were asked to report any health complaint they had now but which they had never had before the death of their baby, or any symptoms which had become much worse since their bereavement. The ten symptoms most frequently reported, all of which are of a psychological nature, are shown in Table 1.

Table 1

MOST PREVALENT SYMPTOMS REPORTED BY BEREAVED MOTHERS

Symptom	Prevalence
General nervousness	31%
Sleeplessness	30%
Headaches	21%
Excessive tiredness	23%
Nightmares	19%
Persistent fears	29%
Depression	18%
Fear of nervous breakdown	17%
Feelings of panic	14%
Repeated unusual thoughts	13%

In addition to the psychological symptoms, women reported health-related changes in their lives. Approximately one in five said that their capacity to work was reduced and that their use of sedatives and tranquillisers had increased. Half of the women who smoked reported a significant increase in their smoking.

Based on the health inventory the women in the study were divided into three groups: those with no significant health problems following their bereavement; those moderately affected; and those with severe health deterioration. Table 2 compares the number of women in the three health categories of this study with the results of research on women who have been widowed.

Table 2

INCIDENCE OF HEALTH DETERIORATION AFTER BEREAVEMENT				
	Numbers of women	*No health problems*	*Moderate health problems*	*Severe health problems*
This study	*110*	*47%*	*32%*	*21%*
American widows	*132*	*43%*	*36%*	*21%*
Australian widows	*243*	*32%*	*36%*	*32%*

The pattern of health deterioration in bereaved mothers is very similar to the two major studies on the effects of bereavement on women after the death of their husband. It may therefore be concluded that the loss of a baby can have as severe effects on the mental and physical health of women as the loss of a husband.

What do mothers say about their grief?

The women in the study were asked to state how intensely they felt their grief reaction was, on a five-point scale of (1) no grief (2) some grief (3) average grief (4) intense grief

(5) worst grief imaginable. The majority indicated that their grief was either intense or the worst imaginable.

They were also asked whether they had experienced the typical stages of grief. Most said that they had experienced the following aspects of grief—shock—disbelief—anger or bitterness—feelings of failure—depression or withdrawal— acceptance of the loss. Not every woman experienced all of the stages, nor were they in any definite order. There is no prescription or clear step-by-step formula to grief. It is a unique, individual experience.

The women were asked how long they had grieved after the death of their baby. It was difficult to get an accurate measure of the average length of grieving because the interviews were conducted over a period of six to thirty-six months after bereavement. However, of the women inter-viewed, twenty-eight said that they were still grieving, and the remainder reported periods of grief ranging from one to twenty-four months. When asked how long they thought most people would grieve after the death of a baby, half the women said they didn't know and the other half thought an average time would be a year—although their answers ranged from one month to forever.

Most women in this study said it took them about nine months to feel comfortable around other people's babies and before they could hold them without feeling distressed. It took about five months to enjoy social outings without being preoccupied with the loss of their baby. Overall the women in this study conveyed that the intensity and duration of their grief was similar to what would be expected after the death of a close adult loved one. They also indicated that the loss of a baby has ramifications throughout the family system, often with alterations within the marriage and to relationships with their other children. It is clearly not an event of little significance as we are conditioned to believe, but a major life and family crisis.

Unresolved Grief

It is perfectly normal for women to experience many of the physical symptoms mentioned earlier. It is also not unusual for them to wonder whether they're normal or if they're going crazy. The death of a baby has a major psychological impact on a woman which can throw her mind and body into turmoil. She may suffer physical symptoms similar to those related to her child's death. She may, at times, find it difficult to believe her child is really dead. She can experience hearing her baby cry, or desperately wanting to hold different objects just to get a sense of holding her lost child. There are times when reality and fantasy seem blurred. Could this really be happening to me? she asks. To the mother and to outsiders, it may seem that she is not coping and is in need of help. Yet within the first six to twelve months all of these extremes of experiences are normal and part of the healthy grieving process. It takes a long time to work through the emotions and reactions which arise from the loss of a baby. The mother needs to experience the depth of her bond before she can begin to let go of the strong attachment. Only then will she slowly recover and enjoy the day-to-day activities of life.

When the physical and mental symptoms persist for much longer than a year and the woman is unable to return to her previous family and social life, then there is a real need for concern. In this study particular attention was paid to women in this category, who seemed to be suffering from unresolved grief.

The women 'at risk' for not resolving their grief in a healthy way were those who had developed severe health problems. Out of one hundred and ten women, twenty-three reported a marked deterioration in their health as well as more social adjustment problems. As a group they had more marital problems. They also experienced a determination not to have any more children based on a fear of a repetition of the tragedy. Overall their reported length of grief was much longer than the other women in the study.

The next step was to try to discover which experienced in these women's lives had made them more vulnerable and less able to resolve their grief. Four major factors emerged which related to women's unresolved grief. Firstly, a crisis during pregnancy seemed to interfere with a healthy grief resolution. So, if the women lose a close relative during pregnancy or have marital or severe family problems, this creates additional stress which must be dealt with. However, as pregnant women develop a psychological immunity, the true impact of such a major crisis tends to be withheld until after the birth. If the baby dies, the woman then has to cope with a double crisis burden.

The next two main factors were whether she felt her partner and family were supportive. Without adequate support from partners and/or family, women were less likely to resolve their grief. The importance of compassionate, empathic support from those close to bereaved mothers should never be underestimated. A grief-stricken woman needs at least one person to listen to her and to understand her. Without this support she will have no choice but to withdraw into isolation more and more. What she needs most is to speak the words that convey her inner experiences to a person she trusts.

The fourth experience that was found to affect a woman's grief resolution was whether she had seen and held her baby. Mothers who had were more often able to reach a healthy grief resolution. It is the reality of the baby and the memories created for the mother that give focus to her grief.

Women should be aware that their experiences during pregnancy and after their bereavement do affect their grieving process. This awareness can help women to make choices that fulfil their needs and will also encourage them to ask or search for support, if it is not forthcoming from their own social network. They need to know that they are not alone and are not the only ones to have felt such anguish. In order for women to complete the grieving process, they need acknowledgement and strength of support from others, and time.

Indications that a woman has not resolved her grief after a year include overactivity without a sense of loss; the presence of psychosomatic symptoms which were not previously present or which have become much worse; major alterations in relationships with friends, relatives and social life; extreme hostility; and unexpressed hostility resulting in a rigid manner. If a woman is concerned that her grief is not being resolved successfully, she needs to seek additional support or therapy. She also needs to know that it can be resolved, no matter how long it has been since the death of her baby.

Longing for what might have been

Monday 20 January
This is the first day without my twin daughters—it is so quiet and lonely. I cannot recall having any feelings; I tried to be pleasant and the nursing staff help, but it is all a front. My milk is in and is upsetting. I can't handle it. I don't want visitors, just my own company; and my husband. I cry and rock myself, look at the photos and have such strong guilt. Sleep is hard to get as reliving is always there.

Tuesday 21 January
Went home 12.00. Tried to get into normal clothes but am bulging with milk. Oh, it hurts, nature is cruel. I leave my room and it seems as though I have been there for ages so much emotion experienced there. By the time I got home I was exhausted. Lay on the bed and cried. My husband was put out when I asked him to hold me all the time, so didn't ask after a while; felt so alone. I feel nothing for my two

sons—they seem to be an intrusion and just too much for me to cope with. Mum tried to be bright and I know it is a front. How I hate it, I want to be miserable, I want to cry, I want to rock myself, I want my girls and I dislike my husband. He doesn't want to talk or show any feelings about losing our girls. Everyone go away. I hate noise. Very little sleep once again.

Wednesday 22 January
Had trouble getting out of bed, even though I have been awake for hours. My husband got huffy because I had quite a lot of phone calls; said he didn't know the callers. I was lucky to have so many concerned friends, but that was only for the first couple of weeks, then they forgot. Managed to do the washing and dinner but nothing else.

Thursday 23 January
Same morning as yesterday. Managed to do the ironing. Still a lot of phone calls from concerned friends; my husband jealous and shouts when I am on the phone, so dread the phone ringing. Janice brought me four baskets of roses; the house was a mass of flowers and perfume. She recalled what it was like when her friend lost a baby, and understood how I was feeling. Another friend, Jan, came to visit and says that I should be thankful for our daughter and the boys, but that is no compensation. Doesn't anyone see that even today they are no compensation. Although I love my children, they still don't take away my longing for my babies. My husband tried to get me to the shops; don't want to go and we have an argument. He doesn't understand I don't want to see people or people to see me. Find concentration bad; can't remember anything, have to write notes.

Friday 24 January
A very bad day. Went to doctor's, felt very light-headed. The doctor seemed to think it was emotion. Got a script for strong Serepax for sleep. Talked to him about how I felt

towards my husband and he related his own experience, when his wife lost their baby at 20 weeks. He sat and rocked his head and said how he had failed as a husband. Couldn't do much today but cried a lot; rocked and stayed in bed. I rang someone from SANDS and just talked and listened. It was good to find someone who had experienced what I was going through and had survived.

Saturday 25 January

Back to the doctor's because I passed out. He still classified it as emotion and told me to take it easy. The surgery staff don't talk to me any more. Can't stand to sit in the surgery, especially if pregnant women there. Don't like people around me, am very conscious of myself and feel people watching every move I make. Everyone seems to have me at arm's length; if only they would acknowledge I am there and treat me like normal.

Sunday 26 January

No emotion, don't converse much, just do what is necessary and lie on the bed. Feel awful. Mad with everyone for being around; just want to 'die'.

Monday 27 January to Saturday 1 February

For first time am on my own with children; can't cope. I manage to do only one thing a day. My husband rings at least once a day; this is the only time we really talk. The days are long and I get weepy, particularly afternoon and evening. My daughter now brings a hanky every time and wipes my eyes. Still won't go out but run out of groceries, so venture to the shops. Met one of the girls from church and when I told her about our loss she said it was 'God's will'. I went numb, thought how cruel and cried. Then she put her arms around me, I know she meant well but that hurt. I thought by going shopping early I would miss people I knew but in actual fact I met a lot. The reaction from some was to play cat and mouse as I walked up the aisles getting my groceries, so that we never actually met. Others acted as though all was right with the world and are over-bubbly saying stupid things like to be thankful you have other children, or try for another. I decided there and then I couldn't go shopping locally again. (I did my shopping elsewhere for four months.) I was too emotional and I cried; made people embarrassed.

All the days are the same, strong guilt, reject my family, except my daughter because she needs me. The others don't. Take each day at a time and think no further. My daughter always cuddles and pats me like a mother, goes and tells my husband if I am crying at night. Jeff is not tolerant of how I feel.

Sunday 2 February

Had another rotten day. Just lay around. Indifferent to my husband and can't stand him. Went back to the doctor as I was still having medical problems, and he said, 'You're O.K.' I suppose he felt it was still all emotional. As I was going out the door he said 'Are you getting over it now, or do you want a script for Serepax or something?' I said goodbye and walked out. I was getting used to being slapped in the face and it just didn't penetrate any more. I had also got to the stage where I wanted to dodge doctors. I felt they treated me as though I was a nut and they were doing me a favour by tolerating my presence.

Monday 3 February

I felt unwell, and didn't think it could all be due to emotion, so I went for a second medical opinion from someone who did not know me. I was admitted to hospital early that morning with severe infection. Throughout this week I would hold and carry the photos and diary wherever I went. It was as though I had something of my twins with me at all times. It upset me to read the diary, but I wanted to be upset. It felt right.

March

I have never felt so out of control in all my life as I have this year.

My husband and I share the same bed and nothing else. I went to SANDS meeting, very upset and must admit I felt I dominated the session, as I just had to talk when I heard these girls had the same feelings and experiences as mine. I was 'normal'.

The film 'Some Babies Die' was screened. My husband would not stay and watch it — went to bed — so I decided to video the programme. I am so glad I did. The next day my husband had the day off and I gingerly said I wanted him to see it. We both sat down together. We talked about the babies and our feelings for the first time, cried and hugged one another, although I held back quite a bit. Had been too hurt to feel free to do this. We also decided to put flowers in the church the week the girls were due.

April
I just existed this month, still numb, not able to remember and concentrate.

May
I felt nothing for anyone; not even my daughter. I could see my spring was very tight. As the twins' due date got nearer, I felt I was going under for the umpteenth time and each time I went under, it was getting longer before I came up. I got desperate and called SANDS. I felt SANDS was the only one I could talk with. We talked for ages and in the end she suggested seeing a psychologist. My first reaction was, had I really sunk to such depths? I had thought of doing something drastic to my life but I hadn't worked out what. Whether I would or not I have no idea but I feel if I had not made contact then, at the rate I was going, another two weeks and I don't know if I could have stopped the continuous slide. I had never been to a psychologist and the only people I knew who had, were people who found life continually difficult.

I did not tell anyone I was going to see her, as I felt I would have more problems coping with everyone's kindness and thinking I was round the twist and strange. When I got to her office, I felt like running out. My spring was so tight, my head ached. I felt sick and cold. I will be forever grateful to her for that time we had, to find her not sitting in judgement, just helping me to spill it all out. There seemed so much to recall, it was like bringing something to the boil (me) and then gradually cooling down. Many tears, I cried for most of the session. But, once I got started, I couldn't stop, there just seemed to be so much shut away inside me that wanted to come out. I had unloaded feelings and words that felt horrible and repulsive things that I could not say to family or friends. That day I drove home, I didn't recall how I got there. I went and talked to a friend and she asked what had transpired and I told her. She said she had wished that she had gone and seen someone rather than try and cope on her own. In actual fact, every time I went to see the psychologist, my friend and I would talk of what happened and how I was going.

June: a very bad month

This was a very tense and emotional time, as this is when the girls were due. I had another appointment with the psychologist. When I got there she wasn't there. I got upset and drove to the beach. I ran up the kerb in the car and couldn't control myself. Banged the steering wheel, telling myself I was stupid and dumb. I had got the wrong day. After crying for a while I got in the car and drove home; it was hell driving while crying. We met the next day. This created a problem because I couldn't ask my friend to babysit; so had to tell my mum and my husband who I was seeing. I had never been secretive, but I held back telling them I was seeing a psychologist, because it was admitting I had sunk to such depths and I was not coping. My mother-in-law, even today, keeps saying I had a breakdown. Both reacted as though they were saying, 'My gosh, she is nuts'. Mum felt it was bad to stir things up; better to try and get on with life and forget. But I couldn't forget. How could I, when my longing for those children was always on my mind? My crying and rocking was occurring quite often again. Wasn't unusual for me to pick up the phone, or answer the door, whilst crying.

By the time I saw her I was a mess and felt as though I was going backwards. So frustrated with myself. The hour we spent together passed quickly, still crying. She suggested I try and set some time aside for myself each day. Also do things I liked. Now, this created problems, because in my house everyone comes first and me second. For mum to say I want to go out and do something was hard for everyone to take. I thought about my interests and found music to be my outlet. It still is.

I found if I set aside one hour listening to my classics and trying to relax, I could cope better. I must emphasise, it was a matter of saying to myself: 'You are going to do this'; it was not something that came easy, but benefits were there, even if only for a short while at first. It was easy to lapse and not put the time aside, so it took quite a while for it to come naturally.

June was an extremely bad month. So many lost dreams. Saw the psychologist again. I find I am starting to rely on this time with her. It is an exploring time; going back many years, and it helps me to understand more about me. The one person I have never considered important but who I have to live with all my life. I became very aware of my feelings, when I am starting to get out of control and get on that roller coaster, when I can't stop. When I got back to mum's I had a cry. Mum asked if I honestly think this is all helping by seeing her. I responded that If I had not gone I would not be there that day. That was a very sobering thought for my mother, who had lost quite a few children. I later ventured to talk about how she was after losing the babies — impatient, hard and too independent, as though she was saying, 'I can cope and don't need anyone to help', because like me, she had been hurt, and didn't want to have that happen again. I told her I didn't want to be like that and felt this was the only way I could achieve a peaceful end to this miserable period of my life.

July

As the time has gone on, I have learnt that if I don't feel right doing something, then I don't do it. Also, if I want to cry in front of someone, I do it. In other words, if it feels right that I say or do something and it embarrasses someone, then it is their problem, not mine.

Since losing my twin daughters I had distanced myself from pregnant women. I found this to be a happy time for them, but a very sharp reminder for me. I couldn't stand new babies for a long time and I would dodge them.

I saw the psychologist for the last time. I came away feeling more in touch with me and vowing to start those one hour music sessions again, which I had let lapse, due to all the pressure. I realised I was so much more aware of my own needs; emotions, how to cope with them and all importantly, what is normal. Even my family now admit it was right I should see a psychologist.

We celebrated eighteen years of marriage in September. If anyone would have told me in February, that my husband and I would still be together, I would not have believed them. To have hated someone so much, but then to say eight months later there was still feeling for that person, is hard to believe. I hope and believe that as time goes on, we will find something deeper between us, something that was not there before the loss of our children. I also have different priorities now. During the first six months I used to live daily and make no plans. I gradually started to plan a day or two in advance. I still basically take each day as it comes. I still have bad days or moments when the tears just flow, but I don't resent them any more. I still took at the photos and kiss my babies and I love them and long for what might have been.

Chapter 3

A special baby

Each baby is indeed very special. When a baby dies, the experiences, the memories and the grief of both the mother and the father are unique. Despite this individuality of experience, some similarities are shared by bereaved parents, both in terms of their reactions and in the circumstances surrounding their baby's death. There are certain aspects that present difficulties with each type of loss.

This chapter addresses the main issues parents face with the experience of stillbirth, neonatal death, the death of one baby of twins, cot death and miscarriage. Similar issues also concern infertile couples, parents who give birth to a handicapped baby, or those who give up a baby, either through adoption, or termination of pregnancy. For each of these major areas of reproductive loss, a bereaved mother's recollections of her own experience have been included. These accounts reflect the essence of that specific kind of loss and the problems encountered by the parents.

Stillbirth

Perhaps the most intense feeling associated with a stillbirth is shock. Certainly, shock is there when a neonatal death occurs, as well. Yet, it is even more so when the mother discovers that her baby has died before it has even been born. This is truly incomprehensible. How can death precede birth? It is like a waking nightmare. One woman recalled how she was told in a hospital clinic that her baby had died. She left the hospital, but couldn't remember anything — her name, where she lived or what she was doing wandering the streets. Eventually, she went to a local police station and they pieced her story together and rang her husband.

She was unable to feel angry, or blame her doctor. Yet it seemed cruel for her to be told so bluntly that her baby had died, without the doctor understanding the emotional impact and ensuring that she had the emotional support she needed. Yet, interestingly, one of the hallmarks of shock is that people tend to look as if they are just fine and coping well — almost taking it matter-of-factly. What isn't seen, of course, is the shutdown of all feelings and in this case the feelings were so overwhelming that the woman's thinking was halted as well. It is a most unusual case. Often the mother herself has an intuition that the baby has died and is more prepared for the words of her doctor. However, this story conveys the intensity of the shock for a woman when she hears that her baby is dead.

The next difficult stage for the parents who have learned their baby has died before birth is the decision-making as to whether the mother should carry the baby until the birth occurs naturally or whether labour should be induced, immediately. If the woman decides to wait, this can be a very distressing time. She may not want to, or feel able to tell many people, and must spend the next few weeks trying to deal with questions and comments about the birth and how happy she must be feeling. She may also worry about whether the birth will be normal; what the baby will look like having been dead for some time; possible danger to her own health and whether she'll ever be able to have a healthy baby. All of these questions need to be discussed and dispelled.

Then there is the birth itself. The nine months of waiting for this special baby, and knowing already, there will be no baby to take home. The delivery room is often filled with silence. Which words can be said? If the mother has known for some time that her baby is dead, she may have begun grieving before the birth. Yet, the father may only really begin to comprehend the loss when he actually sees the dead baby. There may well be a mismatch of their grief reactions at the time of birth, which needs to be understood by each of them.

The reactions of family and friends can be particularly painful in the case of a stillbirth. Compared to a baby who was born alive and then died, a stillbirth may be viewed as a baby who never existed at all. Stillbirth, 'the delivery of a lifeless baby', really says it all. People don't perceive the life and so find it difficult to understand the mourning of the parents in the months that follow.

The mother may experience acute feelings of failure because her baby was not even born alive. She may feel shame and guilt at her perceived failing. This can be made even more painful, when people avoid her, not knowing what to say or do. Many women have said that acquaintances will go out of their way to avoid contact, even to the point of crossing to the other side of the street when they see her approaching. It is vital for friends and relatives to acknowledge that the baby was special and a very real part of the parents' lives. Although the baby may not have been born alive, this does not diminish the reality of its life and the fact that this baby will continue to be a living memory for those parents.

The world did not stop

It's November and the jacaranda trees are in bloom again, their fragile beautiful blossom softly falling to the ground in a shower of purple. My child died and was born on such a day. Can it be six years ago? Yet even now it hurts to put memories and feelings into words.

My son, Robert Michael, was our much longed for third child. (I had suffered a miscarriage two years prior, but that wasn't really 'counted', as I was told at the time.) We had a daughter aged eight, and a son aged six, so we were all quite excited at the prospect of an addition to the household. Extensions to the house were called for, so for months we endured the inconvenience and the stress of tradesmen tramping through the house and the garden being uprooted; not to mention the back of the house and the laundry being demolished, and the first builder choosing to go bankrupt. All was in readiness, however, the week before the baby was born. The nursery was painted and the children helped to scrub the pram and to repaint the family bassinet and the cot. A carry basket, high chair and playpen were borrowed, (as this was to be our 'last' baby anyway) and clothes and toys were in readiness. The bassinet was made up and the carry basket too, all ready to just put the baby in.

One night those familiar pains began. By early morning I figured that it was time to go, so the children were packed off to Nana's and thence to school. They got up at assembly and announced that Mum had gone to hospital to have the baby. Two days later they were up there again, this time to ask for prayers for their baby brother who had died. It must have been terrible for them. . .

During a routine heartbeat check—the baby's heart had been 'as strong as an ox' throughout the day—it was discovered that there was none to be found. My husband and I had no idea that things were amiss, as the nurse said brightly that this often happened. She went off and came back with a senior nurse who also listened in vain. Off they both went and then the room seemed to be full of people, including my gynaecologist. Various monitors were called for and now what only can be described as a growing horror began to dawn on me. I remember glancing wildly around in panic and trying to will that heartbeat to be heard, but all that permeated the silence was my own pounding heart.

'I'm sorry', said the doctor. 'Your baby has died.' What was he saying? I gripped his arm in disbelief: It could not be true, I must be dreaming this!

Then my husband and I were left to collect our wits after being informed that I would leave things up to nature and go ahead with the birth. I was horrified at the prospect. But I couldn't believe it. I kept asking the nurses to check again, to try different monitors. All pain relief was refused as I didn't want to hurt the baby. It was a terrible night. The birth itself was fine, but I didn't want to push him out. Everyone was telling me to push but I didn't want to as he was 'safe' inside me. I guess I didn't want to face the awful reality to come.

By an amazing coincidence, I had read an article just three days before about a support group called SANDS, which was for bereaved parents of babies. It was mentioned how important it was to see and name the baby if it died before birth. I remember reading and thinking how morbid such a group would be. Little did I know that SANDS would be my lifeline in years to come. However, in my shocked state, giving birth to my child, I remembered what I'd read. As soon as he was born, I insisted on holding him. 'It's a boy', said the doctor flatly. 'Is he really dead?' I asked, still hoping it had all been a dreadful mistake. 'Yes', he replied.

There he was, lying silent and still. I suppose that's why they are called stillborn, although that term makes me choke even today. Such a horrible word. He was a beautiful baby, perfectly formed and looking exactly like his sister at birth. No reason was given for his death, except that he died of hypoxia, a lack of oxygen. We never knew why. It has been the hardest thing to accept—whether his death could have been avoided. However, even if we did know, it will not bring him back. It is just something one has to come to terms with.

My husband and I cried then. I was told later that the doctor went out and cried too. I know that nothing in my whole life can ever erase that terrible shock and enormous sadness at what happened that night. The whole scene is indelibly imprinted on my mind.

Later, various members of the family came to see us. Word flew and friends sent flowers and came to visit. It was like a dream. Inexplicably, the children were not brought in until the third day. I shall always regret that they were not offered the chance of seeing their brother. They were angry about it much later and probably still are. We were too shattered to think of it and nobody advised us. It was the same with the funeral. We didn't know what to do. Nobody helped us. Looking back, I realise that we needed the family to help us in that way, but I guess they didn't think of it either. My parents and a close aunt saw Robert, but my husband's parents didn't. Nor were we offered the choice of seeing him again, dressing him or sending down clothes. This has always bothered me and I have been adamant in advising nursing staff and other bereaved parents since, that this is important. The baby should be treated as any other person would be.

I feel that if my full-term baby had lived for five minutes after birth, or had been very premature and then died, his existence would have been given more credence than it was. We were treated just like we'd lost our pet instead of our child. Everyone thought we would 'get over it' in three weeks and of course 'we could always have another one'.

After the flowers had died and the cards stopped coming and everyone around me went on with their lives, the reality began to seep in. I would wake up every morning and immediately remember what had happened, as I had a lot of milk which refused to dry up for weeks. I had to use nursing pads in my maternity bras. It was terrible going through the motions of normal family life. Everyone told me how lucky I was to have two children, but little did they realise how hard that made things. Of course I was grateful and still am, but it was so difficult to look after them, when I just wanted to crawl off to a dark hole somewhere, like a wild animal, to lick its wounds. I still had to attend to their wants and needs, do the washing, cooking etc, and cope with their confused questions that I couldn't answer. Unruly and sullen behaviour followed, for what seemed like months and I felt quite helpless and hopeless in coping with them. My son came in one day and asked whether a fall I'd had a week before the birth killed the baby. I think he blamed me for quite a while for depriving him of his brother. My daughter wouldn't discuss it. I didn't realise that they were grieving too, until one day she raged at me that she wished she was dead. That cut me to the quick. I was shocked. I realised that she was saying that if she was dead I would care for her—like I was caring about the baby. In grieving for my child I didn't have, I was neglecting the ones I did have.

We took the children to the cemetery then, to say 'hello and goodbye' to Robert. This was six months later. It had not occurred to us before then that the children needed to do that. We dressed in our best clothes, made posies of fresh flowers from the garden and took photos of the children near the grave. When we came home, my daughter went to the shed, took out a large flat piece of wood and a hammer and chisel. She worked for some hours. We didn't know what she was doing, but when she'd finished she came to show us. She'd made a plaque, a headstone like she'd seen at the cemetery. We bought a special plant for the garden and put the plaque there.

Long days and nights went by. I felt worse instead of better. I couldn't believe that things around me just kept happening normally when my world had fallen apart. I recall being absolutely amazed on our drive home from the hospital that the traffic lights still worked, flashing from red to green to amber and back again. Some time later, I was out in the garden and I could hear my neighbour bringing in the washing. The pegs were clicking and she was humming. Birds were singing and I could hear the sound of children playing, far off. I looked around in wonder. How could everybody not know what had happened. My baby had died and yet the world did not stop. I felt like shrinking.

Shopping became a nightmare. I really thought that I was truly going crazy. Everybody seemed to be pregnant or pushing a pram. Babies were everywhere. I couldn't bear to be around pregnant women or small babies and avoided situations where I was likely to meet them. Wherever I turned in the shops, there were reminders of the things I would have been buying: baby clothes, toys, food, bottles, dummies, bedding etc. I couldn't walk down certain aisles past those things. Many times I'd have a trolley full of groceries and run out panic-stricken and empty-handed and go home. Or else I'd go to the shop and forget what I'd come for.

My friends seemed to avoid me. I desperately needed people, but I guess I wasn't very good company. I used to sit by the phone and will it to ring. When it did I was overjoyed, even if it was a salesperson trying to persuade me to buy their wares. It was very hard. I even kept on the cleaning lady I'd engaged to help me out before the baby was born, just for the company really.

I found that many people that I expected to support us, didn't, while those whom I didn't, did. Some friends I have not forgiven for their insensitivity and desertion of me then, and I don't see them even now. Others were very kind and I will never forget how much they helped, even in the smallest way, in our time of need.

For a long time I felt that people were staring at me and whispering about me. I felt very uncomfortable in company and for me that was unusual, as I have always been regarded as 'a bright spark who loved being around people'. I hated what I had become and thought I would never be the same again. However, one wise friend agreed that indeed I would not ever be the same after what had happened, as I had been touched irrevocably—like losing one's innocence. There was no going back, but I would get well and although things would never be as they were, they would be as good, if not better. This has turned out to be true.

My family was the greatest letdown. It was terribly unfortunate that my sister and I were expecting at the same time. We have always been a close family and the thought of two cousins being the same age was really wonderful. After what happened, it was a nightmare, not only for me but also for my sister, my parents and the rest of the family.

Ironically, she too had a boy. It seemed too cruel to be true. At first, I determined that I'd be happy about it (which of course I was) and that I would face the ordeal of visiting her and the new baby, which I did. However, it became difficult after a while. Unthinking relatives clucked over him, in my presence, as people tend to do around babies. The worst moment came as I was nursing him one day, feeling very sad, and someone came up and cooed, 'Isn't he beautiful'!! Something snapped inside. I handed the baby back and never touched him again, nor really acknowledged him, until he was over two years old. It has been painful watching him grow up. There is always the shadow of his cousin near him, but he has become a special child to me now and I enjoy his company.

When people didn't acknowledge my pain, that was the hardest thing. If only they'd said, 'This must be hard for you but …' or 'How are you feeling?' I needed to know people cared but unless they told me, I didn't know that they did. My parents' reactions were particularly hurtful. Even now a part of me is still angry and bitter about their seeming lack of support at that time and later, when two more pregnancies ended in disaster; late miscarriages at sixteen weeks. Of course then I was set back to square one, hit rock bottom, and eventually sought professional help. My mother bought my sister a new dress because she'd just had a new baby. Well I'd just had a baby too! Three weeks after giving birth to Robert, my father commented that I was looking a little chubby. Had everyone forgotten so soon that I'd just been through a pregnancy? When I berated my mother on the phone for not ringing me or visiting me, she rang back later to suggest I join a self-help group she'd heard about that was for women suffering post-natal depression!! I remember saying in utter bewilderment that they'd all have their babies, but she didn't seem to understand. I joined SANDS …

Christmas was dreadful and still is. There always appears to be someone missing and there should be extra presents under the tree. As the Christmases go by, I know what toys he'd be likely to be getting. Shopping isn't fun any more really, as I can't help but be reminded. A special candle at that time means that he is not forgotten, although probably nobody else in the family realises.

Anniversaries and birthdays are difficult, especially for my husband, I think. Robert died on Remembrance Day, and one of his extra-curricular tasks at the office is to organise the annual service. We both still crumple at the 'Last Post'. We always make a cake for Robert's birthday and the children decorate it. Some of my family and friends remember and send cards or flowers. This means a lot to us. Birthdays have taken on a whole new meaning. Each is a celebration that you have survived your birth. It is an important occasion.

Time passed, wounds healed, but the house became a reminder we couldn't get away from. The extension mocked us—there were too many triggers of that traumatic time. We both felt restless in that house and without really verbalising why, we half-heartedly started looking around the district for another. We did find one that we liked and it was a good omen that our house sold for cash in the first hour. We were committed then and things moved fairly quickly, quite literally. We've both agreed since on the real reason why we shifted but few people know. I guess they really wouldn't understand. As one of my close friends said six months after Robert died, she'd forgotten about it already and was genuinely surprised when I referred to him one day.

We are settled now. We are lucky, we have two children and they bring us great joy. I have resumed an interesting career and I have a sensitive and kindly boss, who is also a bereaved parent. I feel at ease. There are still bad days or moments, but I live with that. It's always just below the surface nevertheless. My 'new' house has a beautiful jacaranda out the front...

Neonatal death

Premature deliveries make up 70% of all perinatal deaths. The infant's prematurity at the time of birth raises many questions in the parents' minds, as to why this has happened. In addition, they are often called upon to make life and death decisions with some urgency. It may be, in an emergency, that the mother gives birth in a hospital other than the one she had been booked into for delivery. She may have a doctor she has never met before. On top of all of these changes, the baby may be taken to a children's hospital while the mother remains in the maternity hospital. All this turmoil has a nightmarish, unreal feel about it that lingers with the parents throughout the shock.

When a baby lives for a number of days or weeks there are many important decisions the parents must make with regard to treatment or surgery. By far the most traumatic situation occurs when it becomes clear that the infant will not survive. At some point, the parents have to face choosing the time to remove the life support systems.

Mothers and fathers who have gone through this experience describe feelings of both shock and utter exhaustion. The woman is recovering physically from the birth, dealing with emotional trauma, as well as trying to be with her baby as much as possible and involving herself in the decision-making. The father may be working, caring for the other children, providing support to his wife and also trying to be at the hospital to be with his baby and attempting to absorb the medical information about the child's condition. Anyone would find this daunting. Yet, in many cases friends and relatives may not be sufficiently aware of the intense strain on the couple to prompt them into providing the necessary support. It is not usually until months later that the mother and father even realise themselves the horror of that period of their lives. At the time of crisis, they somehow just keep coping and functioning and automatically they just keep going.

At all stages of the hospitalisation of the baby, it is vital that parents receive the support they need from their doctor, nurses and other hospital staff members. So many unanswered questions fill their minds and need to be listened to. Parents remember and value the emotional support they received—the young nurse, who not knowing what to do or say, simply sat with the mother and wept; or the doctor who went to the family home in the middle of the night to be with the other children, so the father could be at the hospital with his wife and baby. These acts of compassion touch parents deeply and are never forgotten.

A vacant place

After four years of marriage, my husband was really keen to start our family. Much to our surprise, I was immediately pregnant and right up until we were on our way to hospital, I had doubts about it being what I wanted, although I knew it was what my husband wanted. After an easy labour, a gorgeous little boy was born and straight away my maternal instincts took over, but somehow I always felt he was more my husband's baby than mine.

When it was time to increase our family, I made the decision and I felt this baby would be more mine. From the start of the pregnancy, I had really bad morning sickness which continued until about four months. After that everything seemed fine. My due date arrived and of course I was late. Eventually I went into hospital to be induced. I went ahead with a very good, 'normal' labour of only two-and-a-half hours. When my son was born in the dimly lit room, he was placed across my tummy and my husband and I stroked him. He was then taken to the other side of the room, presumably to be weighed, etc.

After a while I asked the sister who the other man in the room was, and she told us he would be over in a minute.

The staff had realised the baby was in distress, so had called a paediatrician. He came over and introduced himself and asked did we knew what Spina Bifida was. We had heard of it but didn't know what it meant. He told us our baby had severe Spina Bifida and probably would not live the night. I automatically started screaming 'No', closing my eyes, pulling the sheet over my head. If I couldn't see, perhaps this nightmare might go away. My husband was riveted to the chair, silent. My own doctor was at the end of the bed, silent. He was genuinely stunned too.

I cannot remember too much of what followed, except that it was decided that if my baby was still alive in the morning he would be transferred to the children's hospital by ambulance and both doctors would be back in the morning. The delivery sister was fantastic. My husband went off to tell our families. He went to his parents then rang my sister so she could help him tell my mother.

What sleep I had was really fitful. Each time I woke, I fought to go back to sleep to escape the nightmare and when I woke in the morning my sister was there. I was asked did I want to see my baby but I didn't want to until my husband arrived. I later felt I had rejected my son, but I was really scared to see him. In a way I wished he had died in the night so all the pain would be over! When my husband arrived we had our baby brought in. We held him, cuddled him, cried over him and said goodbye, as he was going in the ambulance.

Later that day we went to the children's hospital to meet a specialist. He said our baby would be paralysed from the waist down, have no organ functions below the waist and he had hydrocephalus. They were sending him for a brain scan. They would know the results tomorrow.

The next day we were told the scan confirmed that our son had severe brain damage. We were told he could be operated on to close the hole in his back and to have a shunt put in to relieve the pressure on his brain. We were to come back on Monday to let the doctors know if we wanted them to operate or let nature take its course; that is, for our baby to die. It was a miracle he was still alive. We were informed of what our son's quality of life would be with many operations; not to cure him so he could live a 'normal' life, the type of life we had expected for him, but just to keep him alive.

We left the hospital that day, having to go away and decide if we would let our baby live or die. It felt like we were on our way to hell. Our doctor came to see us over the weekend. We knew we did not want our baby to have to suffer a life of pain, so we decided that he would not be operated on. That decision was the hardest we have ever had to make in our lives. We were in agony. We went to visit our son each day on the weekend and had our family come to see him. Unfortuately, he was in pain and could not take too much handling, since everyone wanted to cuddle him. We thankfully had this time with him and could include our three-year-old son.

We went back to the hospital on the Monday with our doctor to tell the neonatologist that we were not having our son operated on. That was traumatic. Had we made the 'right' choice? Were we being selfish and not wanting a handicapped child? We truly believed after lots of soul-searching, always putting our son first, that we did not want him to suffer. The doctors assured us they supported the decision we had made.

The following day I decided, in agreement with my doctor, to leave my hospital as I was hardly spending any time there. Leaving a hospital with no baby in our arms, only flowers, was really sad. This wasn't how we dreamt things would be.

One day we decided, with everyone in the ward's encouragement, to bring our baby home for a while. We were nervous and as soon as he started breathing funny we all jumped in the car and went back to the hospital.

During this time I kept thinking about his funeral. I had only been to one before, fourteen years ago, to my father's, and I couldn't get the funeral out of my mind. After a few days of this, I decided we were really lucky he was still alive, so forget about the funeral and just enjoy every moment we had him.

The next weekend was Mother's Day. The hospital made lovely special little cards with a flower and baby's footprint. Just the four of us went on a picnic. At the picnic area, everyone would have thought we were the perfect family, lovely toddler and new baby. Little did they know our hearts were breaking. This would be my only Mother's Day with my two sons.

The next weekend, I was as usual caring for our baby at the hospital, when one of the nurses suggested we take him home overnight. No, I couldn't do that—well maybe—yes, I will. So I loaded up with bottles, medicine, etc., and set off. I didn't want him to die at home, but we knew we could go back to the hospital any time. We kept our baby by our bed all night. We called in to get more bottles the next day. We would keep him one more night. The next day friends asked us to go on a picnic, so we raced to the hospital for more supplies and we were off on a normal family picnic. That too was a good day for us as a family, with caring friends. We are lucky to have friends who cared about us enough to want to be with us, as we were pretty sad company.

I rang the hospital the next day to say I was keeping our son at home. We just had to go in the next day to have him checked and formally discharged. It was arranged for a visiting nurse to come each day to help physically, emotionally or whatever. She was just great. On the Friday night while she was at our home, our baby started breathing funny, so I had her ring around to find out what was happening, until one doctor told her this was how the end would be and that we had had this explained. The nurse asked did I know what was happening, which I fnally admitted, but really didn't want to believe. So, we spent our time watching him. He rallied around and we spent our days caring for him and loving him. We had friends around to see him, which was good.

We had an appointment in the middle of the week with the neonatalogist. Our son was very cold and the doctor told us he was very low. I still couldn't believe he was really going to die. I cried until I shook. We had another doctor's appointment same day the following week and I guess I thought this routine would go on forever. The appointment we made for the following week, however, we would not keep.

The day after the appointment, in the evening, I walked past my baby in his bassinet in the family room; he made a funny breathing noise. I picked him up and he took a few long breaths and stopped breathing. I handed him to my husband and he took another breath, then stopped. We both knew it was time. My mother had been helping us all through the past five weeks and we asked her to take Nathan to bed while we sat and held our baby as he died. We should never have excluded our other son; he should have been given a chance to say his goodbyes.

A long time later he asked why was he not allowed to give his brother a goodbye kiss? We thought we were doing the right thing, protecting him, even though the doctors had told us to include him. Home, after all, was where we felt comfortable with our baby dying. We kept him with us for five hours, just nursing him, saying goodbye. We eventually drove to the hospital where we saw a nurse who knew us and a doctor to complete some formalities. We said our final farewells and laid him to rest in a bassinet.

We drove home silently, had a terrible night's sleep and went back to the hospital in the morning to see the doctor. In a way, we were relieved, exhausted and stunned that it was over. The social worker asked did we want any help arranging our baby's funeral and we gladly accepted her offer. The funeral director came immediately and we discussed options. We suggested a park setting not far from home might be appropriate. We went for a drive and my husband said the park was where he wanted his son buried, because of its tranquillity.

Afterwards, we decided to go on a trip, anywhere, immediately. When we came back from our trip, we tried to get on with life, but our son was never far from my thoughts. I became very short-tempered. I was taking my frustrations and unhappiness out on my three-year-old son. I never realised until much later that he was grieving too, and needed me more than ever; but I was feeling too sorry for myself to help anyone else. I wouldn't ask anyone for assistance because then they would know I wasn't coping.

I took on working with my husband and literally ran myself ragged. The less time on my hands, the less time to think. We started having in-law problems during this time. Mother-in-law didn't want to hear our baby's name, couldn't look at photos, never showed any emotion. We took it that she didn't care. One day everything exploded and we told her how we felt: that by not being allowed to share our feelings with her we thought she didn't care; that she was pretending that our baby had never existed and that was hurtful. We wanted to be able to talk about him—we needed to. She told us she did care, that she cried with other people. We needed her to do that with us. If ever we needed our parents it was now and my husband's weren't there for him. Our in-law problems went on in varying degrees for a long time. Our relationship was terrible and we still feel things will never be the same. Perhaps we expected too much of someone who was unable to cope. But we still felt let down.

I became pregnant again fifteen months later. We had to decide if we would take the risk, as the same thing could happen again. I had an amniocentesis at sixteen weeks, then waited for the results—which came through at twenty-one weeks—technically too late for a termination. Luckily, everything was all right and after worrying constantly for the rest of the pregnancy, a healthy little girl was born. For a while I still worried that she too would disappear on me.

Our life since the death of our baby has had many difficult times. We were lucky that we had excellent doctors to help us advise us and support us. Most of our family and friends were also really supportive, and that was great to know. My in-laws caused us great emotional difficulty but we've learnt to live with that. We all still love our baby son and miss him. There is a vacant place in our family we wish he was here to fill. We have had three children and we love them all.

Single surviving twin

The struggle to comprehend death at a time of birth is even more painful and confusing for a mother who gives birth to twins, to have one live and one die. The mother is both bonding with the new baby and mourning the death of her other child. Emotional extremes become a part of her daily life. How can she be attentive, loving, happy, responsive to her newborn, while she is also feeling shock, sorrow, despair and emptiness because her other beloved baby has died? Every time she sees her live baby, memories of the twin rush into her mind. It is like being torn in two.

Naturally, family and friends focus their attention and conversation around the surviving twin. In fact, if the mother mentions the twin who died she is often met with a cold silence and a quick change in conversation back to the surviving child. She may be 'reprimanded' by well-meaning friends to be thankful she has one healthy baby. She should be happy not sad. They don't understand that the babies are two separate, unique and loved individuals. To mourn the death of one child does not mean the living child is less important or less loved.

The poignancy of this experience was highlighted in our study by the responses of women who had lost one infant from a set of twins. Most felt that it wasn't as bad as losing an only child for they had a baby to take home. Yet as one mother stated, 'It's so difficult to make a bond while letting go. I feel torn in two directions. You are always reminded of your loss. But so few people understand what you're going through that they don't know what to do or say so they avoid you, which is worse.' It is not surprising that many of these mothers experience mixed feelings. 'It's so painful to see her and be reminded of him. I feel really lucky to have my daughter, yet for six months during the time I looked at her I thought of my son.'

Another mother said, 'Yes, I think the experience is different. I have found it very hard to accept the death of my second twin. I found when I brought Ryan home, that I would be doing things for two instead of one. I would wash and change and feed one and then think I'd do it for the other. It was so strange. Even now I look at Ryan and wonder what sort of person Robert would have been, what he would have looked like and whether he'd be doing different things from Ryan.'

We asked the mothers whether they thought their grief would be similar to that of a mother who lost a single child. One mother of twins who had previously lost a single baby at birth said she felt it was different. She said she grieved intensely for her previous child for six months, whereas with the twin who died she thinks of him every day and is still grieving at twelve months. 'I feel split in two,' she said. 'Initially I was just glad to have one baby survive, but I was also so sad to have lost one. I am never super happy like other mothers because I am always grieving.' It is most distressing for anyone to feel both happy and sad, close and distant and grateful and angry. As one mother put it, 'I just feel so confused. I try to be happy and strong for my baby but I feel so sad about the one who died. I just keep hoping that happiness overcomes the grief.'

In most cases the mothers who have lost one twin at birth said they were very close to the survivor. As one mother said, 'He is very very precious. I care for him twice as much, like I prepared myself for taking care of two babies and I just keep it up.'

While most said the surviving twin was very special to them, they were concerned over the baby's health. It seems as if the mother intensifies her bond with the living child and is frightened she may lose this one as well. A few mothers conveyed the difficulties they had in bonding with the survivor. One mother said, 'When I first saw him, I didn't like him and even days later I thought "Well it's not fair he's alive and his sister is dead." But then my paediatrician talked to me and got me to go to the nursery and visit him and all those feelings disappeared.'

Most mothers in the study commented on the need for reassurance from the hospital staff and their need to be told over and over again that the surviving twin was going to be all right. 'For five months I worried and worried about Kim. I really felt she would die too,' said one of the mothers. Another stated that, 'Because psychologically you are expecting and thinking in two, then suddenly there is no longer twins, but one, there is a lot of mental adjusting to do. You really need sympathy and understanding.'

For all of these women, the most distressing experience was the failure of those around them to understand the complex mixture of their emotions. The grief is as real as the joy and both need to be heard and understood.

I often wonder

At first I couldn't believe I could be in labour. After all I was only twenty-seven weeks pregnant. When the nurse confirmed I was in labour and in the later stages, I felt numb What sort of a chance does the baby have? The doctor and nursing staff were preparing us for the worst.

After the baby was born, the doctor discovered I was carrying twins. Both babies were born alive, but in need of very intensive care. They were born in a country hospital with limited facilities. Emotions at this time were very mixed, excitement at having twins, sadness because we may lose them, and hope that they may survive.

Our first tiny girl lived for two-and-a-half hours. We were encouraged to touch and hold her and the doctor made sure some photographs were taken. Our second little girl was taken to Perth for intensive care. The next twenty-four hours were terrible. We had a special little girl fighting for her life in Perth and we wouldn't be with her.

Checking out of hospital the next day was also a difficult time. I felt I was leaving part of me behind; I felt torn between the two babies. The nursing staff had kept us informed of the surviving twin's progress but not once mentioned our dead baby. It was like she never existed.

I sat for hours with our sick little girl and at times I think I saw both babies in her. The time in the intensive care nursery was spent touching and talking to our little girl. Also I was able to talk to nursing staff about both babies. It was difficult at times, but the more I talked, the easier it became, helping me to come to terms with and accept the death of our first twin. I still cried myself to sleep at night and asked myself all those 'if only' questions. Everywhere I went there seemed to be sets of healthy twins and always it brought a lump to my throat.

One of the nurses had told me about SANDS. I had decided to go to a support meeting, but found it difficult to leave our surviving twin and then I began to think, 'Hey, I'm strong, I can get through this on my own!!'

Eventually after five months we took our baby home. It was a very emotionally tiring time. I didn't want to be over-protective of her, but there was still the fear that she might stop breathing. She is now two years of age and has achieved so much; she is happy and really enjoys life to the fullest. I often wonder how they would have developed individually had they both survived.

Some months after returning home, I met another mother who had lost a baby at birth. We spent hours talking and drinking many cups of tea. We found comfort in being able to share our experiences. With the help at the SANDS committee in Perth we were able to start a group in our local community. Being able to talk to someone who will listen and share your experiences is a sure way to heal an aching heart.

Cot death

Couples who have lost a child through Sudden Infant Death Syndrome (cot death) know the tragedy and shock involved in having a completely healthy baby one day and the next day to be holding a dead infant. There is often no indication to the parents that anything was wrong with their baby. Even if the infant has had previous apnoea attacks, the parents believe that it is going to survive. With cot death, the bond is severed in the passing of a few hours or even minutes.

When the baby is found by the parents, the nightmare begins. There are usually extensive, desperate attempts by one or both parents to resuscitate the child while waiting for the ambulance to arrive. If the parents are unsure of appropriate resuscitation techniques, they may later feel guilt and recriminations about being responsible for their child not surviving. One mother told the story of how she was outside playing with one of her other children, as her twins had their afternoon sleep. She had a feeling that something was not right, but dismissed it as being overprotective. As soon as she heard the one twin cry, she knew immediately that something *was* wrong. Racing into the room, her worst fears were confirmed, as she saw her daughter lifeless in the cot. She was a first-aid instructor, and began resuscitation, but to no avail. Months later, looking back, even though she knew intellectually that she had used all the correct methods to try to revive her daughter, she continued to go over each step, feeling that she must have done something wrong. No amount of reassurance from her doctor, or the ambulance attendants, relieved her self-doubt. In addition, she also began to withdraw from her son, the surviving twin. She was so grief-stricken that there was no room in her heart for love for a long time.

There seems to be an endless searching for what might have caused the death. Even more devastating is the parents' wondering if somehow they could have prevented their child's death. 'If only' they had checked the baby sooner; 'if only' they had gone in earlier; 'if only' they had suspected something was wrong. So many unanswered questions can initially lead to self-blame. The parent who finds the baby and tries to revive it suffers enormous pain in the months to follow. However, the parent who is absent can suffer an equally painful time, struggling with the fear that 'if only I was there, I could have saved my baby'.

The trauma of attempting to save the life of one's baby when alone is horrifying. To stay calm enough to take action, while the whole of your inside is screaming with pain and fear, is almost impossible. One woman told of how she began to resuscitate her baby, while dialling for an ambulance. When she got through, the first thing the ambulance officer said was, 'Don't panic.' Somehow, she only registered the word 'panic'. She dropped her baby and stood there screaming until the ambulance arrived. For years afterward, she felt almost unbearable guilt.

Often the parents haven't really known much at all about cot death. Until they speak to their doctor, they may not be aware of what caused their baby's death. They are left in a sea of shock, guilt and sorrow. It is extremely important that the doctor spends as much time with them as they need, to go over all their questions and particularly to assure them that there was nothing they did or did not do that caused the death.

Because cot death occurs so suddenly and in the home, adequate support services are not available to parents at the time and place where they are most needed. The main contacts may be with the police, who need to investigate all sudden infant deaths. Thus, the parents' feelings of guilt and grief may be compounded by the pain of suspicion.

When a cot death occurs, the baby is usually several months old and well known and loved by family and friends. Parents, sometimes, because of their own acute grief, wish to have a private funeral. However, it does seem that the inclusion of family and friends is crucial in helping the parents to resolve their own grief. Also, family and friends who are a part of the rituals and the grief process of the parents are more able to understand the parents' grief. A sharing of these experiences can increase the intimacy and bond with those close to the parents, which ultimately provides them with more support in the long months to follow.

It is not uncommon for parents to want to sell their home immediately, or even move to another city, to escape the nightmare. If they can understand that this is a normal reaction to such a tragedy and if they can receive emotional support, the need to run away may be relieved. It is then that they can begin to face the overwhelming feelings that have arisen inside them.

Our first child

It is now eight weeks since our daughter Ceinwen died of Sudden Infant Death Syndrome. She was twelve weeks old and was our first child. Her death was a great shock to us, but somehow we managed at the time to make a few important decisions that in retrospect have helped us come to terms with our grief a little easier.

At the time of finding our daughter dead, I decided I only wanted the immediate family at the funeral. I realise now, that was my denial of her death and also my guilt that as a mother I had been unable to protect her from death. I also know now that no one is guilty and nothing would have prevented her death. Our general practitioner visited us at home on the night of her death and advised us to invite our friends to the funeral. We took his advice and understand why he made the recommendation. By being with our friends, they were able to express their grief and share in ours too. We needed them there as much as they needed to be there. We also faced them at the time of our crisis, which although difficult at that time, is even more difficult if left till later.

As I'd given birth to Ceinwen at home and had always cared for her myself, I found it hard to come to terms with the idea of an autopsy. But to talk with the pathologist about the results of the autopsy was somehow calming and I tealised that I really wanted to know the cause of her death, and somehow it relieved some of our guilt feelings and answered some of the 'what if's' and 'if only's'. I also felt unhappy about handing my daughter over to a funeral parlour. After all, they didn't love her, or even know her, so would they respect her or would they treat her as just another job? We decided that rather than having strangers involved with our funeral that we'd do it ourselves. The funeral directors provided the coffin and did the paperwork and left the rest to us. We had decided to bury Ceinwen at a small cemetery outside the city. This surprised many people who didn't think we'd be allowed to. It is important to remember that you can choose whichever cemetery you like. You will return to that cemetery often and it's nice to go somewhere you feel comfortable.

We picked up Ceinwen from the hospital after picking up the coffin. We asked the mortuary staff if they would put her in the nightdress of our choice and take a lock of her hair for me, and if they would place her in the coffin. Although I wanted to do this myself, I realised that I couldn't. She wasn't the soft warm cuddly child I was used to and I knew it would distress me too much. It was important to know though that she was still our child and we could choose what to do.

We then took Ceinwen back home in the coffin and had her in the room she had been born in, slept in and died in. It was nice to have her home for a while and to be alone with her to say our goodbyes privately. My sister-in-law asked if she could take her children, aged two-and-a-half and seven years, in to see Ceinwen. I was very unsure about this, but I realised that she made the best decision for her children. They went in and saw her and each of them kissed her and placed something in her coffin. Looking back I realise that my sister-in-law made the right decision. Death is a part of life and it is better if children are allowed to learn about it and to grieve themselves at an early age. If we try to protect them from it as children, then as adults, their grieving might be more difficult.

We then took Ceinwen to the cemetery in our car. We left the lid of the coffin open so that our friends and relatives could also say their goodbyes to her. I felt that it was not only important for me to see her, to accept the reality of her death, but it was important for our friends too. We carried her to the grave ourselves and after the service we lowered her ourselves. Looking back on the funeral I realise that by doing things ourselves we not only gave our child the respect she deserved but also gave ourselves, our relatives and friends, a very private environment in which to express our feelings. Our midwife, who attended the funeral, commented later on how nice it was to see so many grown men being able to shed their tears freely. A relative took some photos of the funeral and also one of Ceinwen in the coffin. It causes me pain to look at them, but it helps bring up some of my more suppressed feelings and it also helps me realise the reality of her death, which after looking at the photos of her alive, is sometimes rather unreal.

Although the funeral directors were very nice, we did feel, as I'm sure many grieving people do, that it's still a business proposition for those in this area. The funeral directors said that we must be at the cemetery at the arranged time. This distressed us as it made us feel that we were being rushed. Needless to say, we were a little late, but the grave digger didn't mind; he himself had lost a child a year earlier. I feel that time to grieve is important and people can wait; it's your time with your child that matters. Another distressing time is making arrangements for the headstone. I don't think anything can relieve this except having previously discussed at home what you would like and thereby arranging this as quick as possible.

At the time of her death I also had a very negative attitude about receiving any flowers. In receiving flowers I had to acknowledge the reason they were sent. The first couple of bouquets brought floods of fresh tears surfacing and looking at them just made me miserable. After the funeral, however, I realised how I appreciated having flowers in the house. They reminded me that there is still beauty in the world. Since Ceinwen's death I've always had a bunch of flowers somewhere, to help cheer me when the dark cloud goes over my head.

At the time of Ceinwen's death I wanted to run away, go somewhere on holiday, sell the house, basically to forget the truth. No matter where you go, you can't escape the reality. The memory and grief is part of you and will go with you. We did, however, spend the night of the funeral at a friend's house. We had a nice hot bath, watched videos, cooked ourselves a nice meal and generally gave ourselves a night off. Maybe this seems uncaring, it wasn't, we just needed a break from our grief. We knew we couldn't escape from it, but we managed to put it on hold for that night.

A couple of weeks after the funeral we went away with my sister-in-law for a couple of days. This was also very beneficial. It gave us a few days of enjoyment; we became sad at times, but not depressed. Having someone with us kept us more motivated, bushwalking, horse riding and generally dissipating some of our built-up energy and anger.

I decided very soon after Ceinwen's death to return to work. I felt that being busy and a part of things would help me come to grips with the fact that life goes on, no matter what. I also needed to be with people and as I work with a lot of people, what better place to fulfil that need. I decided to return to my prior job; I felt although it would be difficult to face those people again, that it would be easier than being amongst strangers. I also knew that it would be difficult for them, they might not know what to say to me or what to do. I asked a chaplain who works with us, if he would conduct a service for Ceinwen at work at the same time as the funeral, so that any staff that wanted to, could join with us at that time. Since returning to work many of the staff have said how much that service meant to them. The chaplain also talked to them about their fears relating to my return to work and they were able to share their fears and talk about how they were going to cope with me and my grief. I feel this has made my transition back to work much easier for all of us. The staff are comfortable about talking to me about Ceinwen and my grief.

Some of the staff still try to avoid me and this is upsetting. I know they're frightened that they might start me crying and not feel able to deal with this, or even shed their own tears. So rather than wait for them to initiate a conversation, I often start things off and let them know that I can talk about my child and her death without always crying and that if I do cry, it's OK and it's very healing. I also took the photos of Ceinwen into work, so that I could share with the staff my beautiful daughter who may not be here physically, but will always be in my heart, whom I will not forget and I don't want to forget and whose mother I will always be.

The birth of a handicapped baby

During pregnancy, it is not uncommon for women to worry at times that there may be something wrong with their baby. When the baby is born, the first concern is that she or he is healthy and normal. The birth of a healthy baby is a time of intense emotions. The parents are joyful, happy and proud and a sense of celebration reverberates throughout their network of family and friends.

When a baby is born with a significant physical or mental handicap, the mother's inner unspoken fear may turn into a living nightmare for both parents. So many conflicting feelings can surface at this time that the joy in the arrival of the baby is crushed by the fear, despair and anger at the knowledge that their child is handicapped. It is not surprising that they often go into a state of shock and emotional blackout. As they let their family and friends know of the birth of the baby the responses they receive often reflect their own feelings. People don't know whether to celebrate or commiserate. Do they come up to the hospital, laden with flowers, baby gifts and smiles, or do they come empty-handed and sit quietly? Some, in their confusion over what to say or do, just stay away.

The dilemma may be amplified when there is a question of whether the baby will survive. There may be days, weeks or months of that unanswerable question, if the baby is in intensive care. The ambivalence of the parents can be heartbreaking. Do they bond with their baby strongly, hoping that love will pull the child through the crisis? Do they try to stay one step removed to protect themselves from the unspeakable pain if their baby should die? Sometimes they feel like the friend who never visits—wishing that they could just run away to somewhere safe and pretend this wasn't happening. But there they are, automatically coping. In a crisis it is natural that we function and do what needs to be done in the outside world, while our emotions get shelved for a future time. With the birth of a handicapped child, that future time may be a long way off. Often the degree of the handicap and the effect on the child's abilities cannot be determined accurately until the child is faced with their developmental steps in the first year or two of life. So the parents wait, hoping and hoping that the doctors were wrong or that their baby is getting better.

The grief that parents experience when they have a handicapped child is unending. One never wishes for imperfection, so from the beginning, their view of the future naturally included a healthy, happy, vigorous child. With every developmental milestone which is not achieved as time passes, the parents' grief is renewed. We all know how proud parents are to convey the first time their child smiles, eats solid food, crawls, stands, walks and talks. And they continue the pride as their child goes to kindergarten, starts school, progresses academically, develops talents in sports or music or art, finishes high school, and chooses a career, a partner and has children. All parents want the best for their children, so when each stage is less than it could be, it is inevitably painful. Parents respond so enthusiastically to their child's achievements. Yet when the steps are never reached or are not achieved for a long time, it becomes difficult to maintain the enthusiasm. This by no means indicates that that child is not well-loved and appreciated for what he or she is. The grief of parents with a handicapped child is very complex—for it is not so much the sorrow of having the child they do have, but the grief over the dreamed-of child who might have been.

One of the most ravaging experiences that parents of a handicapped child suffer from is guilt. Guilt seems to be present, no matter what the diagnosis has been. Parents who discover that the handicap has a genetic cause often feel terrible that they have passed it on, through their genes, to their child. Those whose child is handicapped by birth trauma, usually go over and over what happened and what they and the doctors should and shouldn't have done. Then there are those parents who never have an answer as to why their child is handicapped. All that is ever written on their child's medical file is 'Cause: Unknown'! Their search is even more pervasive. The mother often goes back over the entire pregnancy. Was it something she did? Was it something she could have prevented? Was it because she smoked, drank alcohol, worked too hard, didn't attend to her health, or was it the way she thought? Did she not want the foetus inside her enough, or love the baby enough? The list is limitless. The awful thing is that she probably will never know and may keep punishing herself for something over which she had no control. These parents are left with the sense of 'if only … then life might have been different. Our child might have been normal', and attached to the despair of 'if only', is the anger of 'why me'?

In my years of working with intellectually handicapped children and their families, I was amazed at how they perceived their coping abilities. Mothers who had a handicapped child due to a genetic cause felt that they could cope with that; but didn't know how mothers whose child had been normal and was handicapped due to birth trauma were able to cope. Similarly, mothers of a handicapped child injured at birth were full of admiration for the coping abilities of mothers who had a handicapped child with a genetic cause, or no known cause. What was clear from this observation was that these women who individually had shown such strength in coping, underestimated themselves in their comparison with others. In doing so they demonstrated how much a woman's self-esteem and confidence can be shaken when she has a handicapped child. Our society is geared to normality, and having a normal healthy child is a strong expectation, which in some ways validates a woman's femininity and value as a wife, mother, daughter and daughter-in-law. When a woman has a handicapped child she may feel that there is something wrong with her and that she hasn't lived up to her own hopes and dreams of herself. She needs to grieve not only for the child who might have been but also for the motherhood of her dreams.

Health care professionals often try to assist and support the mother and father by being particularly positive and optimistic about the child's future, and about the parents' coping abilities. While this stance at times may be extremely helpful, it may also be unrealistic—a need to try to make things nice instead of looking at what has happened. When it is conveyed to parents that somehow if they work hard enough with their child that he or she will improve markedly; or that it is not difficult having a handicapped child, the parents may feel that they are inadequate in their own personal struggle. The end result is that they isolate themselves more and more and keep on a happy, coping face for the outside world. Their grief is denied and remains unresolved.

Grief needs to be seen as a natural, normal reaction to loss rather than a sign of not coping. Having a handicapped child encompasses multiple lifelong losses and these need to be spoken of, listened to and understood. No one wants to have a handicapped child. This is not to say that a handicapped child cannot be wanted. It is the impact of the handicap on the child, the parents and siblings that needs to be mourned.

Richard's birth— our life together

Being pregnant with Richard was the best nine months of my life.

For most of my adult years, I had been self-conscious and uncomfortable in my relationship with my body. Pregnancy gave me a physical harmony. My body finally felt integrated with my self. It was intimately comforting to be able to give over to my body's wisdom. It just seemed to know what to do. I was contentedly healthy, intrigued by the miracle occurring within me, and my perfect baby grew.

Richard's birth was the worst thing that has ever happened to me, both in itself and because of what it started.

A catalogue of medical interventions brought to an end our idyllic time together. A syringed drip pumped drugs into my bloodstream to hurry along his expulsion from my body. Metal instruments pierced the birth sac to drain away his warm state of suspension. Painkilling drugs injected through a needle in my spine deadened any warning pain might bring. It was not what we wanted but we believed it was for the best.

And as I laboured with drips and drugs and needles a baby's chances in life were being dashed. His tiny head bashing against a hard bony pelvis that would not yield its opening. Finally, in the ultimate failure of nature and my body, they cut open my belly to rescue him.

He was nearly dead. His brain irreparably damaged. They brought him back to life and I cradled him in my arms in a little cream woollen blanket before he was whisked away to lifesaving technology.

In the intensive care nursery, his brain began to swell. He started fitting two and a half hours after birth. He fitted on and off, his body alternating between lifeless floppiness and surging stiffness for the next five days.

The doctors gave us no hope. They discouraged our quest for positive signs. They told us he would be severely handicapped. I didn't want to know. Nor did I want a handicapped child.

It felt like our son was being constantly attacked, condemned to worthlessness. He was no good. He had failed. But he was our son. We defended him. It was all we could do. We rallied behind the best we ever dreamed he could be. Our contact with the doctors almost always seemed antagonistic. They were determined that we should accept their reality.

A few days after Richard was born, the physiotherapist who had taken me for my antenatal classes came to see me. She was from the time of expectant healthy babies and maternal fulfilment. The contrast between what we thought would be, and what became, was too much. I cried uncontrollably. She didn't come again.

I was braver for friends and family. Lots of people sent flowers, some visited. It took real courage to face us with a visit. They didn't quite know what to say. Neither did I. There was no sense of celebration for Richard's life. What else could you do?

I felt proud of myself when the hospital staff recognised and reinforced my cheerfulness. I was beginning to master emotional self-control. But they put me in a room on my own at the end of the corridor, just in case.

Richard regained consciousness six days after birth. He took my breast milk from a bottle that day and on the seventh day, I fed him myself. Love overflowed with my milk. The miracle had happened. He was coming back to life. I remember being overjoyed when he uttered his first whimpered cry.

We went home from hospital only two weeks after Richard was born. The doctors had warned us to expect a hospital stay of at least two months. His remarkable recovery added fuel to our optimism. We rejected prophecies of gloom. As far as we could see, Richard had come through unscathed. We had been spared. He was going to be OK.

And so it was for the next couple of months when evidence of normality required him only to feed and yawn and kick and turn and raise his head. But when the tests inevitably started to get harder, the spectre of disability threatened again.

He wasn't responding to objects, he wasn't interested in exploring and discovering his world, he wasn't sitting up, he wasn't crawling, he was frequently, inexplicably agitated and distressed, his head was growing too slowly.

'Unfortunately, slow head growth means slow brain growth' the doctor said. 'And you can see for yourself he's slow in developing'. That was it then. Reality.

At twelve months, he started to get sudden jolts through his body—quite out of the blue. At fifteen months, he started to have fits again. They have continued with varying degrees of intensity ever since.

Our perfect baby died again and again, with each new diagnosis killing off our latest relationship with him. The doctors had been vindicated.

He had a paediatrician for his body, a neurologist for his brain, a physiotherapist for his mobility, an ophthalmologist for his sight, a psychologist for his behaviour. All of them entitled to make observations and judgements about our son and about us—what was wrong with him; what was wrong with us, as parents; whether or not we were coping. They scribbled notes as they observed, sent reports between themselves and made our lives busy and purposeful with appointments.

At first my excuse was being busy with a new baby. Then I was busy with doctor's appointments. Being busy as a distraction became my constructive obsession. There was no feeling, just activity, and no emotional nourishment to remind me just how much I needed it.

Mothering a handicapped child is a lonely isolating life. Friends with careers had trouble enough understanding the demands of normal motherhood, let alone those of mothering a child who was not normal. Nor could I join easily with other mothers of young children. There was nothing I could contribute to talk of baby achievement or share in the marvel of human development.

As babies crawled around the floor and were delightful at new mothers' groups, I would be frantically trying to calm Richard down as he arched his back and thrashed his limbs in distress. It was his protest against any disruption to the predictability and security of his routine. He didn't enjoy outings. He hated unfamiliar people and places. I was getting that way too.

When the other children gave up their dummies, Richard's was indispensible. Chomping furiously on a dummy was the only thing that seemed to deflect his agitation. On the rare occasions I thought beyond today, I despaired at the picture of me trying to calm a great thumping child with an oversized teat. These days his dummy is well and truly a thing of the past. He bites on his hand or clothes, or chews on his toys instead.

Reproduction was popular in our families around that time. As grandparents, uncles and aunties clucked over cute toddlers, they were all too well aware of the poor, sad comparison with our little boy. They felt guilty about being enthusiastic for their children's achievements. It hurt them as it hurt us.

Over the years, my shell became very brittle. A sense developed that if my sadness was not contained, its enormity would overwhelm us all. It felt like if I let anyone come close to me, to touch my sadness, the tide would break beyond redemption. Little by little I shut down. My reports of Richard and our life were well rehearsed and unemotionally factual. Of course I was coping.

Seven and a half years, and a lot of personal growth and therapeutic support later, I am closer to my feelings. I well up with tears easily and unashamedly. It is manageable. Every now and then I go to pieces for a while, usually in response to some new crisis or disappointment. When the fitting gets bad or his behaviour suddenly becomes uncontrollable, I give in to myself and then I recover. I know I can put myself back together again.

As I look back I regret the loneliness of my grieving. No one cried with me. No one has ever offered to share my grief—not my husband, not my mother, not my sister, not a friend. It has only ever been me on my own. Perhaps I made it hard for them, and I know I never asked, but I was too weak to appear vulnerable.

Richard is a very compartmentalised part of my life, at night and on the weekends. Weekdays, I go to work.

He is a very pretty little boy. The severity of his handicaps is not immediately apparent. He lives and loves passionately and demands unlimited supplies in return. He takes and talks and tries so hard to give. He grapples and fumbles in a world of incomprehension but listens and attends and tries to communicate back to us. We love him with all our hearts as any parents do. We thrill in his achievements and acknowledge the contribution of his life to ours. But, more often than not, our life together is very, very hard.

Most of the time we spend at home, with him watching videotapes of 'Play School' or 'Young Talent Time'. Sometimes I accuse myself of laziness for not taking him out more, but I know I am also frightened of bringing on the ferocity of his resistance to change, or his frustration at not getting his own way when he can't communicate it to us. Occasionally, he will walk happily to the park with me. I sing songs to him all the way there and back. More often, he fights and bites as I duck and run ahead of him.

We don't go on holidays as a family any more. The last time, he struggled desperately as we sat confined for hours on our journey. He was frantic by the time we arrived at our destination. That night, he fitted continuously for three hours. We couldn't find the doctor. We couldn't stop the fits. Finally, what we feared might be an overdose of Valium, worked. I kept thinking he was going to die. We came back the next day. It was such a relief to be home again.

We look forward to going back to work after the weekends. At work, I am a professional, competent woman. I am challenged and rewarded for my achievements.

At home, I am an often inadequate, uncertain mother who copes fairly well, most of the time.

I go ballroom dancing on Wednesday nights to a place where I have no identity other than as a rhythmic body and a pair of feet.

Just occasionally, my worlds overlap and someone from my other lives will see me at the shops or some other public place, struggling to be Richard's mother. I feel like I've been caught out, unable to feign the confident carefree self they know me as. If I can get away with it, I will look the other way and pretend I haven't seen them. If acknowledgement seems inevitable, I will rush my hello past them. It must be obvious I'm embarrassed.

Saturday morning shopping recently, Richard was very distressed for some reason we couldn't work out. We were walking together when suddenly, he would grab hold of my hair at my neck, and yank my head down to his. He did it several times. It hurt terribly. My first inclination was to lash out, to hurt him back. I just kept saying as firmly and calmly as I could, 'Richard, let go'. Other shoppers stared, of course. I hate people to see me so exposed. I keep eyes downcast, terrified of the confrontation between their feelings and mine.

No matter where we go there is always the knowledge that we are very conspicuous and that people whose attention has been called to us are making their own judgements about Richard's life and about what they would do in our situation. It's not a simple matter of shrugging it off, confident that you know better, because you don't. When your experience is such a lonely one, other people's opinions seem to matter.

Before Richard was born, we talked of having several children, a family of children. I thought three, my husband wanted five.

Richard is still our only child.

Many's the time I've accepted our subsequent infertility as a blessing. There has been much conflict and pain between us over the years. Our fights over Richard's management are full of accusation and self-justification, with each of us wanting to convince the other of our own uncertain prescription. We try our hardest, we want for the best, but rarely acknowledge it in each other.

We have been through a lot together. We are still together. We would both like more children. It has preoccupied me more and more this past year or so with the growing realisation that Richard's only-child status has not been good for him or for us.

I am now thirty-five. Our infertility has been diagnosed, in part as due to damage my body very likely sustained during Richard's birth. The problems are not insurmountable, and there is a good chance we can conceive another baby without detracting too much from nature's role. I have been undergoing treatment for the past three days. I should know whether it worked, whether I'm pregnant again, in a couple of weeks' time. I daren't hope. There is such a long road ahead.

Miscarriage

The profound grief of losing a child may also be felt by women following a miscarriage; their loss as intense and long-lasting as that experienced after a stillbirth or neonatal death. The accounts of women who have miscarried convey the depth of their sorrow.

The loss of a baby up to the twelfth week of pregnancy is termed a spontaneous abortion. Neither of the terms 'spontaneous abortion' nor 'miscarriage' convey the reality that the mother has lost a baby. When it is realised that 10–20% of all pregnancies end during this period of gestation, it is possible to grasp just how many women in our community are affected by these losses. Emotionally, the first trimester seems to be the period when the mother begins to experience the baby as an integral part of herself. For this reason, if the baby dies during this term, the woman may feel that she has lost a part of her own self. Grieving over the loss of one's self can be as painful as grieving for the loss of the real baby outside the mother. Of course, some women will not be as profoundly affected by a miscarriage as others. It really depends on the meaning this baby had for the mother. Certainly, when the mother loses a baby that has been her wished-for infant, then she can be deeply wounded and vulnerable.

The most difficult problem faced by women who have had a miscarriage is that they have nothing tangible to grieve over. There is usually no baby to see, hold and touch, no funeral and no memories to keep. Added to these feelings of emptiness is the fact that legally, a baby is not even considered to be a baby until the twentieth week of pregnancy. Therefore, the woman has no validation in the outside world of her loss. Friends, family and health care professionals may consider the miscarriage as just a minor event, probably not even a loss. Because no one recognises and acknowledges the extent of her loss, the woman may attempt to discount or disregard her feelings of loss and grief, as they arise.

Following a miscarriage, the mother can experience grief responses similar in duration and intensity to those of women who have had a perinatal death. She may be particularly prone to feelings of guilt about her inability to carry a baby through to life and she may go over and over in her mind what she did or didn't do to cause the miscarriage. Again, there is the need for her doctor to be sensitive to all her worries and doubts and to reassure her that it was not her fault. She may feel jealous of other women with babies and try to avoid them. Some women doubt their ability to bear a child and in some ways grieve over potential future losses.

Care givers, family and friends need to acknowledge that a significant event and major loss has occurred in the woman's life. She should be encouraged to express her feelings and talk about the loss of her baby, for she is, in reality, a bereaved mother.

A place in our home and hearts

When I became pregnant for the fourth time I was so happy and excited. It was September and in February of the same year we had had our third child, a beautiful daughter. We also have two older sons. I had wanted this fourth child very much. When the pregnancy was confrmed I imagined who it would look like, its sex, where it would sleep, a few names and I even prepared some baby clothes.

Sunday afternoon (the eleventh week) My morning sickness became worse. Rob teased me, saying 'Not morning sickness, again?' I replied 'Yes' and he was happy, as he had guessed I was pregnant a while ago. This was our last child and we couldn't wait to see and hold it.

Thursday morning We rang everyone and told them. I also rang for an ultrasound as we both wanted to see if I had a feeling of wanting to see if it was OK. I had also a sudden feeling of not ever seeing it alive. Rob said not to worry, it would be fine. Mum came over with a toy animal.

Friday afternoon We have our ultrasound, the doctor says only six weeks gestation (eleven and a half weeks by my G.P.'s calculations). A sealed letter to our G.P. told come back in ten days. Rob reassures, I must have been out in my dates; I know I am not! I am a little worried.

Saturday evening A sharp painful contraction. Straight to bed.

Sunday morning Went to the toilet, dark red blood. I shuddered at the reality of what was happening, rang Mum, and she looked after the kids for the day. Mum reassures me she bled with me; if I just rest in bed it will be OK. I rang King Edward Memorial Hospital and they said it's quite possible I may miscarry.

Monday morning Saw my G.P. Took sealed letter— didn't want to see contents of it. By this time I'm pretty upset; I really didn't want to know the reality of what was going to happen. 'Go to bed and rest.' Rob stayed home, and I went to bed. A friend, Michelle, came around 4.00 p.m. with a bouquet of flowers and tried to cheer me up. Later in the afternoon I suddenly realise the inevitable is going to happen. The pain becomes stronger, I ring our G.P.—meet him at K.E.M.H.

Around 5.30 p.m., the most incredible, strong, labour-like contractions one or two and it was all over. I was standing in our doorway! I told Rob, he and I both have tears in our eyes and we drive to K.E.M.H. By this time I was bleeding heavily. Whatever happens now, I think, I must try and see the foetus. The nurse was very kind but I think she found it hard to understand why we were so upset. After all we did have three other children! She was very kind and sensitive and explained everything to us. Our G.P. arrived, and explained that the baby was dead and he'd have to get a specialist in. By this time I felt pretty angry. Our G.P. gave a sympathetic smile or remark and I bit his head off.

'Why did this happen?' I needed some reasons and answers. Was it the shock of my schoolfriend dying the same week? Was it my rigid dieting? Was it because I didn't bother to go for a proper ante-natal check-up? I felt guilty as I had been very blasé about my physical care in this pregnancy. Why? Why? My doctor says one in five pregnancies abort. I was just unlucky. True, but little comfort Why me?

The doctor came. He said, 'There's no baby' What are you saying, I had a pregnancy test, I had an ultrasound, I saw it, what do you mean? I searched my handbag to find my ultrasound picture, only to realise it was home under my pillow. 'Blighted ovum'. What's that? Explanation. Technical jargon! Not able to absorb. All that penetrates: No baby. What does he mean? After all those hopes, all those dreams, there's nothing to see aftcr the D&C I lay back, dejected and stunned.

I was very dizzy and bleeding a lot. 7.00 p.m. Up in the trolley to the ward to get ready for theatre. I lay there quietly until just after 8.00 p.m. and had my pre-made. I couldn't fight the injection and I didn't really care. Down to theatre, the doctor was late. I had in my mind all this time even if I lose this baby I want to see it. Now there was nothing, I couldn't believe it. I woke up in a state of shock or really nothing. No baby I mumbled, no baby. Rob was there wondering what I meant. He had to go home when the specialist arrived, to look after the kids. He left me to sleep it off.

Tuesday In the morning Rob arrived trying to be cheerful. We quietly left, leaving behind something we had wanted very much.

I started the little amount of housework with a vengeance. Rob became annoyed and told me to rest. I ignored him. We went by to pick the kids up from my friend's house. She patted me gently. I felt so angry and hurt. I really ached inside. The kids were happy and seemed unaffected, which annoyed me, but I was also glad they were not traumatised. Later in the week I became more angry and upset. (I cried on and off for a short while.) Memories of my nursing days echoed inside: 'You'll get over it' 'It was only a miscarriage' 'It was probably for the best'; 'Cheer up you can have another one'. Other ladies in retrospect seemed in shock too.

Thursday I went to my G.P., cried for the first time in front of him, and told him I couldn't understand why I was so upset, as I had heard so often it was only a miscarriage. He explained it was because the baby meant so much to me, and to give myself time. I was glad I was going back to see him next week. He gave me reassurance that I wasn't losing my mind.

Saturday I got drunk. Rob had to reinforce I did lose the baby, as I in my state, kept on thinking, hoping it was a dream.

Tuesday I hurled abuse at Rob, accused him of not wanting it, and he justifiably hurled abuse back, saying he did. I went to bed. He took over the kids. I ached so badly, a real physical ache in the heart. I thought I was going mad. I took some Mogadon and went to bed and when they wore off, I took some more.

Thursday Saw my doctor. I had lost weight and wasn't sleeping. I looked dreadful. I had never been this thin. I was so angry. My G.P. said 'I understand how you feel'; I said 'How could you possibly!' and I was so mad and then I burst into tears. Whenever I was reminded of the miscarriage, I started to shake in the hands and legs. This lasted about six to eight weeks.

I also found it extremely hard to see my sister-in-law as she was pregnant and due around the same time as I was. I felt as though they didn't really understand and it was a special time for them. I just couldn't cope seeing her pregnant. I wish I had told them how I felt, as we didn't see or hear from each other very much until their son was born. I think it was hard on everyone. I found it too hard to talk. My mother also felt sad as it was her grandchild too. I really wasn't very good company. A few of my friends couldn't understand why I was feeling this way, it was hard on my family and friends too. For me it was better to stay away for a while.

By January, my fifth pregnancy was confirmed. Though happy and wanted, it brought feelings of concern and worry to last my whole pregnancy. At seven weeks I bled again, similar again, off again to K.E.M.H. to do an ultrasound. Was this to be a repeat performance? I cried quietly when I saw Jamie's heartbeat (relief!). Whenever shock or surprises came I worried until the day Jamie arrived—the healthiest of them all!!

This experience has been like a death and grief process for me which eased a lot after June 8th (my expected delivery date). I have never gotten over this. You never do I suppose, but I have come to terms with it. It has made me more aware and less awkward of people's feelings of death, and generally stronger as a whole person. I see people in a different light than before.

We bought a tree on my expected delivery date to signify a place in our home and hearts.

Relinquishing motherhood: adoption and termination

Women who choose to terminate their pregnancy, or to give up their child for adoption, may experience similar psychological processes in coming to the decision not to bear or not to keep a baby. The similarities also extend to the subsequent grief frequently experienced by the women who have made this decision. Furthermore, mothers who decide to relinquish their motherhood undergo the same grief reactions of sadness, loss or guilt, as do mothers who have suffered other reproductive losses. A decision to relinquish motherhood is difficult for many others to understand, and it may be particularly painful and difficult for someone who has lost a baby through neonatal death or miscarriage to understand that a mother who has given up a child in this way may feel similar grief to her. The unique pain of this loss, and where it differs from other experiences of losing a child, is that if the woman later regrets her decision, she may feel overwhelmed by guilt and shame that the loss of this child was by her own choice, rather than something beyond her control.

When a woman considers whether or not to keep her baby, there are many factors which she will need to weigh up. Perhaps it is this complexity of issues that places such a heavy burden on some of these women later in life, and impedes the resolution of their grief. A woman who becomes pregnant and chooses not to have her baby may feel this as a major life crisis, with all the concomitant internal conflicts. Often her decision is related to the timing of the pregnancy. It may be that the woman is very young, and without the support of a stable relationship, or in a relationship which would end if the baby became part of it. She may feel that she lacks the financial, emotional or social support to even begin to imagine coping on her own with a baby. She may be a victim of rape. She may be carrying a baby with foetal abnormalities. Whatever the situation, she will need to consider all of the reasons for and against her decision. The balance of the pros and cons may be very close. The closer it is, the more difficult the final decision will be. Also the closer the balance, the greater the possibility that she may regret her decision at some future time.

Despite the difficulty and complexity of the decision to give up a child, there is little compassionate understanding of the dilemma of these women. Society perpetuates the myth that a woman who decides to relinquish her baby or terminate her pregnancy makes a free and informed decision, choosing between equally adequate options. This is rarely the case. Often the woman feels that she is in a no-win situation, without a choice. A freely made decision implies that the decider has reached a crossroad, with each path equally attractive. Frequently, in these situations, it seems more like a crossroad where one path is to the survival of the self, and the other heads over a cliff into the unknown. For an individual to take on the responsibility of parenthood is an enormous step. To become a parent when one has no partner, no social or family support, no money or no stability is terrifying, and would test the resolve of even the strongest person. And yet society paints a picture that the choice reflects only the woman's feelings about her baby, and that a woman who decides to give her baby up for adoption, or seeks a termination, is selfish, or unable to love. In reality, the woman may feel that she can neither materially nor emotionally provide well enough for herself or the child, and that to bear the child, or to attempt to care for it herself would be unfair to both. Outsiders may see this view as inaccurate, or unrealistic, without appreciating that this is how the woman experiences her position, and that she cannot make her decision on the basis of any experience but her own. Therefore, a woman may carry through her life the great burden of believing that she actually had an equal choice about her baby. Usually this is not true. The woman may carry this secret pain that she was totally responsible for this decision, without recognising, or having others understand the complexity, and the imbalance of the choice which she was asked to make.

The other myth which has been perpetuated is that the bond between mother and baby begins at birth. This has been a convenient justification for society's insensitivity to the grief of women who relinquish a child or have a termination. Since there has been little acknowledgement that the bond begins at the point of conception, women believe that what they are entering into is a purely logical and physical loss. No one speaks of the inevitable grief. Because it is often unspoken, women frequently deny the reality of the pain they feel underneath. The focus on the physical loss to the exclusion of emotional and psychological losses may be mirrored in the medical treatment of women. They may be dealt with in a cold, clinical fashion in environments which are equally unemotional and antiseptic. These experiences scream out to the women that there is no emotion attached to their decision. They validate society's myths and invalidate the women's inner pain.

A woman who has a termination in the third trimester of pregnancy due to foetal abnormalities can go through a most horrendous time, often followed by a longstanding grief reaction. This is particularly the case with older mothers who have awaited their baby with great anticipation and who are running out of time to have another child. Medical staff also find this type of loss very difficult. The doctor, having been instrumental in the decision for the pregnancy to be terminated as a result of the findings of genetic tests, may then find it difficult to mourn and share the mother's grief. Hospital staff may lose sight of the fact that the mother's grief is over the loss of her wished-for baby. Therefore it is essential for them to understand the mother's experience and listen to her feelings.

Given the magnitude of the possible effects on women's physical and mental health, it is surprising that only in recent years have the effects of relinquishing a baby or termination begun to be investigated. The findings generally show that women may suffer long-term psychological problems and are at risk for unresolved grief reactions. These women may also be more prone to problematic relationships with men and with their future children. Clearly, it is essential to provide adequate services for women who are considering adoption or termination. Such services should incorporate information and education to assist women to make informed decisions, and counselling to assist in the decision process. Needless to say this counselling must be nonjudgemental, without moral prejudices and non-directive. A woman must have access to someone she can trust to explore her feelings and discuss her dilemmas. The alternative of bottling them up and locking them away only causes future problems for her and those close to her. It is also essential for a woman to understand the early bonding which occurs between a mother and her baby and to be aware of the possibility of experiencing grief, shame, guilt, anger or other emotions.

For years women who have experienced the loss of a termination or giving their baby up for adoption have kept the secret of their inner pain. They have been afraid to talk to their partner, afraid to talk to their friends, afraid to talk to their priest or minister, and there has been good reason for their fear. Society has made harsh and punitive judgements on women who have made these decisions, forcing them to feel ashamed, to keep their decision secret, and to feel that they alone have made this choice. Statistics, however, tell a different story. Approximately twenty percent of Australian women of child-bearing age have a termination each year, an experience they often have to face alone. About two thousand women relinquish a baby for adoption each year. Not all of these women will experience grief, but many will, and of those who do, the majority will be expected to grieve alone and in silence.

Emotional scars

It has taken fifteen years to finally start to come to terms with the physical and emotional scars left with me after the adoption of my child.

During that time I have let only a few people really know me. I guess I didn't really want them to come too close. I was suspicious of anyone who wanted to have a relationship with me. Always doubting their motive and expecting them to turn away from me if they found out I'd had a child.

Within the past two months I have found out some non-identifying information about my son and I also discovered my address on the birth record was the unmarried mothers' home. The anonymity shocked me. I guess I always thought that if he had wanted to find me, the record would have been there.

For a long time I believed that I didn't want to meet my child—only recently called 'my son'. I had totally cut myself off from the memory. Every day I know it had happened—physical scars reminded me of that. I always thought if they were not there, everything would have been OK and I could really have put it behind me. I was told many times not to think about it and to get on with my life. I believed that I could.

In fact, until recently I thought that I hadn't really been affected and wondered why some women in a similar situation were such emotional wrecks. Now I knew that I was profoundly affected, but had blocked it out almost completely and compensated for my inability to love by committing myself fully to a career.

Looking back, I realise that I was a very rebellious, very active young girl who was highly competitive in sport and constantly seeking accolades for my achievements. My family and I lived in the country and there was plenty of room for fun and adventure. I don't remember ever feeling bored.

At fourteen, my father decided to take a job in the city and I was optimistically looking forward to the adventure.

When we arrived, I quickly realised the big city was a totally different way of life. We moved to a townhouse with a small back area, not even room for a dog. I was unable to take up my sport because there were no adequate facilities at school or anywhere close.

I compensated my need for adventure by getting to know the 'bad' crowd at school. It didn't take long to be accepted by a fairly radical element of young kids in the area. I enjoyed the nonconformist attitude of the group and wanted more freedom to see them. My parents strongly disagreed—so I began to sneak out to meet with the group and became interested in a boy.

The sneaking turned into wagging school. I was having a great time, thoroughly excited by the freedom. However, this ended when I was caught by the school. Facing expulsion and my parents' disappointment, I decided to run away.

It wasn't hard to convince my boyfriend, he had enough money. We travelled around and ended up in another State. I was eight months pregnant before I decided to go home. My picture had been in the paper occasionally and I was scared of being caught by the police. I had also begun to worry about how I would look after the child, after it was born.

My boyfriend and I had a fight one day and I rang my parents and told them I was pregnant and wanted to come home. They didn't hesitate at all, they wanted me back home as fast as possible. My parents were wonderful to me. I don't think I was really conscious of much of what was going on. I just wanted them to take over and make the decisions.

Back at home, the enormity of my situation began to create a huge panic in me. People began to talk about adopting the child out, as it would be the best thing for me and it, and I would be able to get on with my life. It was a very emotional time. My mother had aged ten years from the worry. My father must have found it incredibly hard, faced with a fifteen-year-old pregnant daughter.

During the first eight months of my pregnancy, I believe I blocked out any feelings of approaching motherhood. I didn't really comprehend what was going on. The whole time I'd been away I had had no support of a close woman. I didn't even see a doctor until my eighth month and remember some vague plan to go to the hospital to have the baby when the time came.

My parents decided it was best for me to go into an unmarried mothers' home until the child was born. They said they wanted to protect my younger sister. The home was the most depressing place imaginable. It was awful. Nobody wanted to be there and the nuns made us work all day. I remember really wanting to go home so much.

Each week all the girls in the home trouped off to go to the hospital to see our social worker and doctor. Everybody was relinquishing their child—there never seemed to be any alternatives.

My parents worked very hard to stop any contact between my former boyfriend and myself. It must have been an awful time for him. I don't remember giving him much consideration.

My father had decided to take a job in another State and they wanted me to go with them to start my life again. It was a rosy picture, leaving all the trouble behind.

The social worker was pro-adoption. In fact I don't really remember any alternatives. I know my parents would have helped me with a flat, had I wanted to stay where I was, but they wouldn't have taken me and the baby with them. To my fifteen-year-old mind, the best thing for everyone was for the baby to be adopted. I asked questions about the adoptive parents but never really got anywhere. I kept clinging to the optimistic belief that it was the right thing to do.

When the baby came I remember being in labour for twenty-three hours. My mother stayed with me. It was a huge relief to have the epidural block. They gave that to all relinquishing mothers.

The system worked well if you were giving a child up for adoption. I was in a ward with girls from the home—we were all relinquishing. I remember the horror stories going around: 'If you look at the baby you'll never give it up'. I was absolutely terrified of seeing my child and wanting to keep him. But not even being able to give him a decent home, I saw my life ending and thought I would have been a dreadful mother. By this stage, I didn't want to be with the father. The drudgery of being a poor sixteen-year-old mother with little financial support was too unbearable.

I was in hospital for five days. I never saw my child. On the last day, my social worker came to me with the adoption papers. She explained that I had thirty days to change my mind. She did go into some basic explanations of the adopting parents—that they had been well screened and were good people. I remember feeling very trusting of the system. I believed them totally. I had no choice. I signed the papers and went home with my family. I was given some shots and tablets to stop the milk flow, put on a diet and encouraged to do plenty of exercise.

Every day I thought about the countdown time to change my mind. I know I wanted to but it was impossible.

The baby was never discussed again.

We moved interstate and I began to make plans about what I wanted to do. In the beginning I told new people I met about the adoption, but after a while realised that nobody understood or knew what to say back to me. I realised that boys thought very differently about me if they knew. So I began to keep it to myself.

There has not been a day in the last fifteen years when I have not reminded myself that I have had a child and that I am different from other women. As the years went by, my perception of what people would think if they knew began to distort. It is like having an enormous black background. I began to feel that no one could ever understand, or really know me, without the judgement that I was a terrible, wicked person, who gave her child away!

I did get my life together and threw myself fully into a career. I was very successful. I was never able to have a normal relationship, though. My real feelings of myself were always endorsed by the type of men I chose to be with. They were usually married and unable to commit to me in a long-term relationship. I know I always felt lonely and wondered if my life would ever be fulfilled with a partner or child. I have had friends who were important to me, but none who really knew the truth.

When I reached thirty, I began to realise and admit to myself that I wanted more from life. I started to think more about my child. I wondered if I would ever find myself in a long-term relationship. My doctor suggested that I see a psychologist and try to deal with my past.

During the last ten months, I began to look at the me trapped inside. I have gone through some incredible changes. I can see how much time I have spent denying my feeling about relinquishing my child. I have always felt different from other women and had very little time for what I considered weakness in either sex. When each relationship broke up, I felt it was inevitable—I didn't see myself as the sort of person who should marry.

One of the biggest steps I have taken is to register my name and details with the knowledge that someday, he may want to meet me. Even though this is extremely painful for me to think about, I know I am beginning to get in touch with the truth about how I feel. It has taken me fifteen years to talk about my losses. It is like peeling back a thin layer at a time and learning to live with a little bit more exposure.

The best thing is that I am finding out that the few people I tell are not judging me. In fact, I have found out that so many people have been affected by adoption. I am not bitter towards anyone. I know my parents did the best they could, and have always loved me. The system to deal with people in my situation was wrong. There should have been some form of counselling for all concerned.

Even though I have never seen my son, I feel a connection to him. I grieve for him. My feelings are very deep and painful. I know one day we will meet, but only if he wants it. I wish him a joyful, happy life, filled with love and peace and hope that one day he will understand my story.

Talking at a deeper level

When I was confirmed pregnant with my fourth child I was ecstatic. My husband took a few days to get used to the idea, as he was quite happy with his two boys and one little girl. I knew or thought this was to be my last pregnancy. I was not well from the beginning of this pregnancy, but nothing I couldn't cope with. We had worked out where the baby would sleep, etc., as our house is only three bedrooms and once this was worked out I could see no more problems.

At nine weeks I started to bleed and was ordered into bed and from there I was told to go to a general hospital. The reason for not going to a maternity hospital was because I was not classed as really pregnant and very easy for a D.&C. for the doctor. This hurt and still does. After four days in there I had an ultrasound and the baby was alive and correct size, etc. I was ecstatic. I was sent home to take it easy, which I did, but it was very hard with three young children.

At eleven weeks, I started to bleed again and was ordered back into hospital. I hated this place as no one knew anything about maternity care and I felt I was a real nuisance. Everyone wanted me to lose this baby so that their problems would be over and I hated them all. After a few more days another ultrasound; this time it showed I had been carrying two babies—one was lost, the other was fine. I was stunned. I don't know if I was sad or happy; both I think. At least my baby was still alive. I was sent home again to take it easy and from here on I was mainly in bed. The pressure was on at home. My children were confused, my husband was angry to be in this situation and I was angry as well. But at least my baby was alive and growing. I just went one day at a time. My baby to me was everything. My whole future.

The final week of my pregnancy was spent in hospital. The doctor called in another specialist and together they told my husband and myself that if they did not take my baby I would die. I didn't really believe them. They said 'You are only 19.4 weeks pregnant so it doesn't really matter. Your baby isn't really real yet, but at 20 weeks that's different. Then you have real problems. You must do something now. You have three days to make up your mind.' I hated the lot of them and I really just wanted to die with my baby. My three children were brought in that night—the eyes of my son went right through me He was pleading with me to get well. I knew what I had to do. For my husband the decision was easy to make. I could make it only because of my other children needing me alive.

I had to transfer to a maternity hospital. The staff there were marvellous to me. I wanted to see my baby but I just didn't know what she was supposed to look like and they said 'Your baby is a real baby and will look just like a real baby. Would you like to see your baby?' I didn't think that was allowed—I thought they would just throw her out with the rubbish and God that thought was killing me. When I told my husband I was to see my baby, he was really angry but I told him I would see her anyway. As it happened he came in and took some photos of her and together we cried and touched and held her. I told her how sorry I was; my guilt was enormous and even now this is still with me. This is the part I would do differently. I would have tried to have really caressed her, not just touched her. I wanted to really love her but I was scared, what of I don't know. I needed to love her as I loved and held my other babies. Because of her non-existence according to the 'law' I guess I felt a freak for wanting to do these things. I would love to have another chance to right these things. I was asked if I would like to see her again and although I wanted to, I felt I was not supposed to, so we said goodbye to her and they took her away.

The staff gave me the phone number of SANDS to call, if necessary, when I got home. Looking back I think I was in some form of shock and the reality of it all, the real loss, the real guilt, the anger, anger, anger. I couldn't talk to anyone for fear of being rejected again and so I just worked and worked around the place. I was incapable of any warm feelings for anyone, not even for my children. In fact they just seemed to get in the way. My head was already full and I couldn't stand their intrusion. After a while, I decided I was quite mad and needed help, so I phoned the SANDS number. I then saw a psychologist and she helped me to throw out life lines to my husband and also one of my sisters. I had to tell them of how I felt; this was hard, but their reactions were not what I had expected. My husband did hurt, he did cry, but his coping mechanism was different to mine.

Looking back I think the things that people have said have hurt so much like 'It's OK you can have another baby' or 'You already have three healthy children, just be thankful for that' or 'Did I read about such and such in the paper—wasn't it terrible, just be thankful you are not in her shoes ...'

I have come to realise that I am not mad, that I am entitled to feel whatever I feel even if it is not what everyone else wants me to feel. If I feel angry I am angry. If I feel miserable, I am. I try to be honest with my feelings, although it is sometimes very difficult, especially to share feelings, as most people either say the wrong thing or reject you altogether and this makes me very angry. I am learning now to pick the right people and the right occasion, but I still make mistakes.

I am always trying to be the same person I was before I lost my daughter, but I think if I am honest I never will be. She changed my life and because she was such an important part of my life it is impossible to be the way I was.

It is over a year ago now and I know I am better than I was, but at times it hurts so badly. In the first twelve months I found myself not being able to concentrate and in the middle of saying something my mind would go completely blank. I am getting better now; it still happens, but not so often.

The anniversary of my daughter's death was due and I was in a panic. I had nowhere to go to remember her, as she legally did not exist and so had no grave or memorial. My need to visit a cemetery was enormous so I went and wandered around one searching for a grave with which I could identify. I found peace there. I didn't have the right to kneel down at any particular one, but at least I could feel sad and cry and remember with pain, the day my daughter was taken away.

In the very early days I made sure I never had any quiet time. I worked around the house and never gave myself any time to think about my daughter, or grieve. I have always loved music, but because it used to upset me I never played any. Music still makes me very vulnerable but I now find I don't fight these feelings—I just let them go. It still makes me sad and sometimes I find it hurts too much, but more and more I find I can endure it quietly and sadly and sometimes I can even enjoy it.

I guess I had become a great actress. The best way to describe my moods would be so high that once alone, I was exhausted. These highs were very hard to control and happened in a group situation, or where I was expected to be in control. If these people saw me alone, they would never realise I was the same person. The second mood is the 'pits' where I get very depressed. I want to run away. I hate everybody and I object to doing things for anyone. These moods upset the whole house but I can't seem to control them either. The happy medium mood is what we would class as 'normal' where I can actually feel peaceful inside. I can love freely and play happily with my children and be totally happy. At first all I had was the highs and the pits, but now I can achieve happy medium and not even realise it is happening.

If anything positive could be said of my daughter's death, it would have to be how she has changed my attitude to the children. They have been exposed to a very angry mother, which I feel extremely sorry about, but on the other side, I am trying to encourage them to share their feelings. If they feel rotten—fine by me. If they get angry and throw their toys around I let them go. I talk to them at a much deeper level. They see me angry, sad, loving, the whole lot. I guess my children would know me best of all—with them I am not vulnerable. I guess because their expectations are not the same as adults. I show them I love them more often and I try to show them good as well as bad.

Having been exposed to death at such a young age doesn't appear to have had any harmful effects. They have cried with us and they have asked hundreds of questions about death and dying. I have answered them to the best of my ability.

The pressure on this little family has been enormous and I can easily understand how losing a precious baby like ours could wreck a relationship. We have had a constant battle ourselves, as feelings such as anger and hatred were something new to me and I didn't know how to deal with them. My husband still can't understand how I can hate him so much and yet still love him.

Today I had an experience which left me devastated. I did not realise how vulnerable I still am. I obviously cannot take any more hurt directed at me. Something happened today which hurt me to such an extent I became a crazy woman. I screamed and yelled and was so full of anger that it was necessary for me to belt the pillow. I belted and belted until I was exhausted and then cried and felt so utterly useless—a complete failure. I felt I was really crazy. Afterwards I felt extremely tired and just rested. When my husband came home I felt so much better for being able to tell him. He didn't criticise, he just listened and agreed with me, 'Yes, my love you are crazy'. He understands and that makes a huge difference.

We have just had the third anniversary of our baby's death. After the first time, instead of waiting for it to happen and then not being able to cope with all the feelings, I spent a special day of quiet and was able to deal with the feelings as they came. Although it does not always happen that way, it is so important to me to feel my feelings rather than push them away, so that they eventually erupt like a volcano.

On the anniversary date I still feel cheated, as I cannot go and place flowers on my baby's gave. She does not have one. All I have of my baby are the precious photos which my husband took. To the world, my baby never existed. She was not entitled to anything—not even a birth certificate.

When I was attending SANDS in the very early days after our loss, I could not understand why mums were coming back to SANDS years after their loss. I did not foresee that the grief could possibly last for such a long time. Now I am in that category myself and I realise just how long the whole process takes. I am coming to terms with my life as it is, but my baby will always have a very special place in my heart.

Since losing our baby, I have found myself repeatedly slipping back and although I know what I could be doing, I do not always do it. I guess that is part of being human. Although we know what is needed, we think we are different and will be all right. This assumption is very wrong, as I have found out.

Over the past three years, as my children have been growing older, I also came to resent them and blame them for the loss, as it was for them that I made the decision to terminate my baby's life. I have had to seek professional help in this respect and am now at least learning to love them as they deserve to be loved. When you love someone, I guess you are totally vulnerable and it is a hard thing to allow oneself to be vulnerable after being hurt so badly.

Infertility

Infertility is probably the least acknowledged loss in our society. The grief is often faced alone. Infertility is truly the death of a dream. So many hopes and dreams of the couple are gradually ended. When two people plan their life together, they have both individual and shared views of their future, which often encompass having children and being a family. For those in their early years starting off as a couple, there is a sense that the world is their oyster; that their dreams will become focussed over time, and life choices will be safely in their hands.

In our society couples may delay having children until they have achieved financial security. A young couple's hopes may begin vaguely, but take shape over a number of years. Thus, although their children are only a distant reality, their present decisions are often motivated by their future dreams. Foundation stones such as saving money, establishing a first home and developing social relationships with couples with children or planning to have them, all set the scene for their dream to unfold. Many years of dream preparation can be involved.

When the couple decides to have a baby and this wish is not fulfilled, it can impair their present life, and the whole foundation of their relationship. Like a pebble thrown into a pond, the ripples spread in all directions—present, past and future. When you really listen to the experiences of infertile couples, the extent of their loss becomes clear. When children are a part of their life's dream, so much needs to be mourned: the loss of the babies they longed for, the loss of all that children bring to a family, the Christmases, the birthdays, the joy of watching them grow and develop. They are robbed of the experiences of being parents, and painfully and repeatedly reminded of their loss when they share in these joys with the children of friends and family. A wished- for child brings into a home a new focus and new life to loving and being loved. So, when infertility becomes a reality the couple can lose their sense of direction in life.

These experiences are quite different from those of couples who consciously have chosen not to have children, for they have created their dreams with different ingredients. In our society, where it is now more common for couples to choose not to have children, it is understandable for family and friends to assume that the infertile couple has chosen this path. The couple, feeling particularly vulnerable and sensitive to questions of pregnancy, may opt for the easier answer of saying that they have chosen not to have children. In one sense they try to protect themselves from probing questions, yet at the same time, they distance themselves from the understanding and support they may need from others.

If they decide to speak of their infertility, they may not necessarily receive the empathic understanding they need. The depth of grief experienced in infertility is difficult for others to comprehend. The paradox of this loss is that there is no one to mourn. When a couple has lost a baby through stillbirth, neonatal death or miscarriage, emotional support, even though minimal, may be received from family and friends. However, with infertility there is no baby to focus the couple's sorrow, or that of their family and friends. Society emphasises the outer, physical and tangible world, implying that to feel loss, we must first have had something. The inner world of hopes and dreams of what might have been is readily dismissed.

In Australia, one in every ten couples of child-bearing age has infertility problems. There are three main categories: primary, where pregnancy has never been achieved; secondary, where subsequent conception is difficult; and repeated miscarriages, where a woman is unable to carry a baby to a live birth.

With such a high proportion of couples in our community with problems of infertility, it should be something which can be talked about openly. Yet it is not easy for couples to discuss their feelings, for infertility seems to have a stigma attached to it. The issue is shrouded in myths that need to be challenged. Often people assume that infertility is psychological and dismiss a couple's real medical problems as being 'all in the mind'. Another mistaken belief is that anyone who is not pregnant does not really want to be. Usually following this line of thinking is a suggestion that if the couple proceeds to adopt a child, then a pregnancy will occur automatically. Although we have all heard of such cases, they are no more common statistically than pregnancies with infertile couples who do not adopt. Finally, when all the platitudes are exhausted, the couple may be told that it is just as well they cannot have children because of the need for zero population growth, or the state of the world. Such responses naturally alienate the infertile couple and they speak only tentatively of their inner feelings.

As a couple faces infertility, many emotional issues need to be dealt with in order for the relationship to survive and be healthy. Initially the partners may blame each other for the failure to conceive. Later there may be self-recrimination and guilt about comments made or questions asked, or bitterness and resentment at the deeply felt hurt. Then, if it is discovered that only one partner is infertile, there may be guilt at the thought of depriving the other of the opportunity to have children.

Infertility may be extremely painful for a woman whose self-concept and self-esteem are linked to motherhood. In our society, pregnancy can be seen to validate a woman's sexuality and worth as an individual. Thus, her self-image and confidence may be threatened by failure to become pregnant.

Just as having a child may be necessary for a woman to feel complete, so infertility may threaten a man's self-image. This is especially pertinent if he is the infertile partner. For many men, the loss is easier to bear if the woman is infertile. The inability to 'sire' a child may leave him feeling less masculine; less of a man. This can relate to his wish to perpetuate part of himself, through the tradition of having a son and heir. He may also feel shame, and harbour doubts about his sexual attractiveness and worth. He may fear that his partner chose him not only as a lover, but also as a potential father, and that if he is unable to fulfil this role, he is less lovable, less valuable, or less sexually attractive. He may then fear that his partner may turn to another man. Issues such as these may be felt less distinctly and a man may be aware only of a sense of emptiness. If he can talk openly about his feelings—and for many men this is exceptionally difficult—he may discover a sense of loss for the opportunity to care for, protect, teach, and rejoice in his own, special child, bringing to bear the particularly gentle masculine aspects of his capacity to love.

For both men and women, children can reflect important but vulnerable aspects of their inner selves. The pride, joy and love which parents feel in their children are often emotions which are difficult to feel about themselves. One of the many gifts which children bring is a special awareness of these precious and sometimes all too rare feelings. The tragedy of infertility includes the loss of this possibility.

The complex emotional issues associated with infertility have been further complicated by advances in medical technology which increase the chances of conception. Some of the better known of these include in-vitro fertilisation (I.V.F.), artificial insemination by donor (A.I.D.), and gamete intra–Fallopian tube (G.I.F.T.). Couples who choose to investigate these and other programmes may find themselves dealing with a daunting array of complicated technical information, and the prospect of further raised hopes and disappointments, not to mention a barrage of moral, ethical and emotional questions which will place additional stress on their relationship. These pressures on their relationship may include the intrusion of technology and rigorous preparatory programmes, or the emotions which may arise if a woman conceives a child which is not biologically that of her partner.

Infertility has the potential to trigger a sense of loss, both within each individual and within the relationship. Such an intense emotional exposure to an empty search may leave the couple with few resources to meet the threat to their relationship. Counselling is often necessary to assist infertile couples through their emotional traumas. In many places, support groups for infertile couples are being formed, which provide opportunities for people to be listened to and understood. Such groups can be a source of information, emotional support, and acknowledgement that others, too, experience the same losses.

Finally, it is important for friends and family to appreciate that infertility is a major life crisis, and to be able to listen to, and understand it as such, even though the loss is not physical, and the wounds cannot be seen.

One ordinary day in August

Time has been both friend and foe. The three or four years when I was completely engrossed by the infertile experience are recalled with sadness.

For me, children always seemed to be a part of my life. I adored them and often preferred them to adult company. Growing up in a large family and playing mother to my younger sister, all seemed natural. When I chose teaching as my profession, it seemed a logical and comfortable selection.

I spent the first part of my married life swallowing the pill and hating it. As we departed for a six month overseas holiday it was such a relief to know that I could throw the packets away. But as our holiday drew to a close our anxiety levels rose rapidly. What we had always presumed would happen immediately, just didn't eventuate. Obviously something was wrong, but what? We automatically accused each other. The word infertility was just not part of our vocabulary. We felt confused, bewildered and unprepared. So we tuned to the medical profession to look for the answers.

Things grew progressively worse as the years slipped by. With every interview, investigation and hospitalisation, many possible answers were given. Together we sought the advice of at least six different specialists. We were put through intensive screening. The daily tests, pills, charts, injections became all so consuming. Slowly infertility became an inescapable disease spreading through body and mind. We felt angry, frustrated, hurt and grief-stricken. Emotionally we spiralled downhill. We searched the reasons why we were infertile, why we wanted children and why we needed to stay married. Then slowly over the weeks I became aware of a tight cramping feeling in my stomach. I still remember thoughts of suicide, though thank goodness, they were no more than light flirtations. When finally I mentioned my thoughts and symptoms to my husband he recognised them as signs of depression, much to my surprise. That evening we plotted a change of direction in life.

Several goals were formed; to buy a house of our own, take a holiday, etc. I knew that I was in a state of limbo and that the only way out was to fight. Passivity was not the answer. I had lost control of my destiny, lost confidence in my ability, in so many areas. I had stopped living. I was reduced to thinking constantly about myself, my inadequacies, my bodily functions, my regulated sex life, my surprising inability to cope with my see-sawing emotions, and my failure to be the perfect wife, daughter and daughter-in-law.

Slowly I started to climb out of the bottom of the barrel. Several things accelerated the climb. Firstly, my husband's unfailing attitude that he loved me for what I was and not as the mother of his children, together with our mutual determination to enjoy ourselves and plan our future. Secondly, my own attitude had to change—I wasn't a worthless piece of humanity. I could make some contribution to society. Thirdly, I needed to know that I wasn't the only female on earth incapable of conception.

By coincidence I saw an article in the newspaper one day entitled 'Infertility'. Carefully, I cut it out and kept it. A week later whilst driving to work I heard a talkback programme on the same topic! I couldn't believe it. A few days later I mustered the courage to phone the contact person. The conversation that flowed generously was to change the next three years of my life. 'Concern' a self-help support group, was about to be launched. I was invited to come along to a meeting where a doctor would speak on infertility. For moral support I asked a friend to accompany me. I remember the uneasy feeling of being so conspicuous and I also remember just how normal-looking the people were who sat next to me. The room wasn't full of freaks after all! That's the ironical part of infertility, you don't display your handicap, like broken limbs. Instead, your injury is within, unseen, but every bit as real.

As the years passed I became involved in the running of 'Concern', and the new field of in-vitro fertilization. It was important for me to make contact with other couples to see just how they coped. I also found great solace in reading articles on the topic. My family and friends could not provide the kind of support I needed. My family was anxiously awaiting a precious grandchild and friends were enjoying their new roles as parents. I felt alone and alienated.

My husband and I looked long and hard at the alternatives to pregnancy—childlessness, A.I.D., I.V.F. and adoption. For us, childlessness was just too painful to consider. My two attempts at I.V.F. were enough to make me view the whole process with cynicism; the emotional drain, the low success rate, the high cost and the dehumanising procedures. We embarked tentatively on an A.I.D. programme. However, a funny twist of fate landed me in hospital with a ruptured endometriotic cyst. The end result was two blocked Fallopian tubes. At last, after eight years, I had a reason for infertility. Somehow the knowledge was sweet. Thankfully, I was spared the uncertainty of raising an A.I.D. child.

Adoption was a possibility, though not a definite one. From the time we placed our names on the waiting list we thought little about it. Six years of waiting and not being able to get a response from the Community Welfare Department rather dampened the enthusiasm. Then, on one ordinary day in August our adoption happened. For a few days before we took our daughter home I was in shock. Once again the unexpected, the loss of direction and long-term plans. Did we really want children after twelve years of marriage?

This time we shed tears of joy. Our daughter was to prove more than we could have hoped for in a biological child. We cannot adequately express in words just how much happiness she has given us.

The years of grieving for our own biological children have ended. Although physically I shall never be able to conceive a child, I can now live comfortably with that knowledge. Time has been a patient teacher. We have grown wiser through the years of pain.

Chapter 4

What do bereaved mothers need?

In order for the bereaved mother to resolve her grief, she needs as many memories of her child as possible.

Mourning is a process in which all our thoughts, feelings and memories of the dead person need to be gone over and over inside ourselves. When an adult loved one dies, there are so many experiences to draw on—literally millions of internal memories. It is all of those experiences of the person, all the photographs in our mind which we review in great detail, that assist in our grief. We have memories of the way they looked, their special characteristics, their laugh, their smile, their beliefs and values, their strengths and their weaknesses, all the times we have shared with them. We have a need to look back over our internal photos of our loved person.

A mother whose baby dies has so much to grieve for and so few memories to assist her. This is why maternal bereavement following the death of a baby is the most complex and difficult form of grief. It is not surprising that bereaved mothers often cherish the few experiences and mementos they have. A photograph, hospital bracelet or lock of hair can be so precious. Such limited experiences and reminders of a beloved child are greatly valued. Women are grateful for any experience which to them validates the reality of their baby. Anything that states that their baby really did exist is vital. One woman told of learning that her house had been burgled while she was out. On hearing the news, her first question was. 'Did they take my baby's photos? They are the only precious things I own'.

Hospitals and professional staff are becoming more aware that women need to be given the opportunity for these experiences and must not be robbed of them. Normally, the difficulties in maternal grief are exacerbated if the mother has not had the opportunity to see and hold her baby or be involved in decisions regarding her baby. When there are no real memories, no internal photographs, then a woman's grief loses its focus. The feeling of emptiness and nothingness becomes pervasive and it is this uneasy and anxious void that makes women wonder if they're going crazy. Reality becomes difficult to define.

When the father, other children, family or friends have seen the baby and shared their experiences, it makes the baby seem so much more real for them all. A link is formed. This link is important in the long term, for women to be able to talk openly with their family and friends—for in a sense it is as though they have 'known' her baby too. If neither the mother nor any close family member ever saw or held her baby, there is a lingering feeling that perhaps the baby didn't exist. Everything becomes a haze. It is this sense of emptiness that is so disturbing and causes women so much anxiety. The experiences of touching and holding her baby, the visual memories and significant linking objects all assist the mother to mourn her loss.

Each woman needs to make decisions to suit her own needs, her own beliefs and her own personality. Just as there is no right or wrong way to grieve, there is no prescription for the most beneficial resolution of grief in the future.

Unfortunately, many of the major decisions need to be made at a time when women are still in a state of shock, and therefore finding even the most minor decision difficult. There may or may not be a lot of advice available, but the most accurate guide is within the mother. She knows better than anyone exactly what she needs to mourn the death of her baby. If she can find some quiet time to be still and listen to her feelings, then she will know what needs to be done. Her internal guidance is the most trustworthy. In many cases women feel very rushed in making their decisions and often hospital staff, for their own needs, may wish all the details to be sorted out. Women should not have to hurry their decisions which are important and may need time.

For the women in our study, the most important experiences in aiding their grief included:

1. Seeing and holding the baby

Over half the women in the study had seen and held the baby after death and none regretted doing so; whereas all of those who had not done so expressed regret that they had not.

There seem to be three main reasons why women have not seen and held their baby.

Firstly, some hospitals or their staff do not offer the opportunity to women, or it is offered in such a way as to invite a negative response: 'You don't want to see your baby, do you?' There is still the mistaken belief that if the baby is whisked away unseen and not mentioned, then the mother will not be as upset. This is often a sad indication that staff are unable to cope with their own feelings about death. If the staff involved with the care of the mother are not comfortable about the idea of holding the baby who has died, then it is impossible for them to reassure the mother.

A second barrier to a mother deciding to see and hold her baby is a feeling that it is a morbid thing to do. In our society there is a taboo about touching a dead person and yet, it is one of the most natural acts we can do. To touch and hold and be with a person we love is not unnatural, sick or perverse. It is healthy, normal and helps so much in comprehending the reality of the death.

Thirdly, particularly where the baby has suffered a deformity or is disfigured, the mother may be afraid to the child. Her worst fears are that she has given birth to a 'monster'. Yet neither I nor anyone I've spoken to in this work, has found that the mother was repulsed by the baby. The fear is only in the imagination and sadly remains there if it is not challenged by reality. Even children with quite severe deformities are seen in perspective and the beauty and uniqueness of the child comes as the main focus. The mothers are able to detect, as only mothers can, the finest detail of their children, who they look like in the family, and their own special characteristics.

The staff involved must be caring and respectful when they show the child to the parents. The baby should be dressed and wrapped in a blanket as with a live infant. Again, the demeanour of the staff can enhance or detract from the experience of the parent.

Having a suitable place where the mother and father can spend time with their baby is important. Ideally, a hospital needs a 'Quiet Room' which is solely allocated to bereaved parents. The place should be homely and relaxing and not a clinical, formal room. The room should be designed so that there is a bath and changing table, so that the parents, if they wish, may bathe and dress their infant. It needs to be quiet and secluded so that the parents are not interrupted or intruded upon. Parents need to have as much time as they wish with their baby; there is no time limit to saying goodbye. Parents also need to have the opportunity to be with their baby as often as they wish. It could be that they initially spend a short time and the next day wish to spend hours; whatever feels right for that family is right.

If the parents want their other children, close family members or friends to see their baby, this should be possible. Again, the quiet informal atmosphere allows a more comfortable and natural experience for the children and family. The shared experience provides an important foundation for the future health of all the family.

2. Naming the baby

One hundred and two women in the study named their
baby and none regretted doing so. Three of the eight women
who did not name their baby regretted not having done so.

The fact that so many women named their baby is a
reflection of how important this act really is. Just as we would
not consider referring to a widow's deceased husband as he
or it, we need to speak of the baby using the baby's name.
Using the name conveys our respect and belief that the baby
did exist and was special. Certainly, in grief resolution
therapy, to be able to refer to the baby by name assists the
parents in their grief, for every time we speak the baby's
name, we bring to the mother's mind and to our own an
image of the baby. The more real the baby is made, the more
the grief can be expressed.

3. Photographs

In our study, in 40% of cases, a photograph had been taken
of the baby and given to the mother, and every mother was
glad that this had been done. Where a photograph had not
been taken, all mothers regretted it. A majority of women
thought that a routine hospital policy of keeping a
photograph of the baby on file in the hospital, accessible to
parents if they wished, would be appreciated. Even if the
mother does not initially want the photograph, she may
return at a later date to have it given to her. Women treasure
that photograph of their baby as it helps them remember and
validates the baby's existence.

4. Funeral arrangements

Where they had the opportunity, half of the women in the study had been actively involved in making the funeral arrangements and a similar proportion attended the funeral. All the women who had attended the funeral were pleased they had done so. Of those who did not attend the funeral, approximately one-third regretted not attending. Some of the women stated they would have liked more assistance with the funeral arrangements from hospital staff.

For both the mother and the father, it is very difficult to make all the necessary funeral arrangements, when they are in a state of emotional turmoil. Often the parents may never have experienced a death in the family and may know little about funeral procedures.

Sometimes, well-meaning family and friends assume that it would be in the mother's best interests for them to make all of the arrangements. Some women have said that their family had not only made all the arrangements, but had not informed them of the funeral until it was over. The family's intention is undoubtedly to protect the mother, but in fact they have robbed her of a very significant ceremony that would have helped her resolve her pain. The needs and wishes of the mother and father should be the highest priority in each decision. Otherwise regret and resentment as a result of their lack of involvement may persist for years.

The parents need to know they don't have to rush. The decisions don't have to be made immediately. The mother may be recovering both emotionally and physically and she needs more time to be involved in the decisions and to be able, if possible, to attend the funeral. The options to be considered by the parents require consideration after the initial shock and confusion have subsided.

Parents need to be aware that there are several sources of advice and support around them. They can request information from their doctor, the social worker, minister, hospital chaplain, funeral director, or the SANDS organisation. Although parents may receive advice and information from various family members or professional staff, the final decisions must be consistent with their own beliefs, needs and wishes. There is no standard prescription for the most appropriate funeral rituals. Wherever possible, the mother needs to be involved both in the arrangements as well as in the funeral. It provides the mother with a sense of completion of her baby's life; vivid memories which she will be able to recall throughout her life. Parents often find that a funeral or cremation service gives the death of their child the importance it should rightfully have.

5. News of the baby's death

Most women indicated that the news of the baby's death had been broken to them in a way that they would have wished. They reported that the person who told them showed empathy and compassion and that the news was given in an honest and straightforward manner at the earliest possible time. There was a preference to be told in a private room and for the parents to have the opportunity to talk to their doctor or nurse afterwards.

Where mothers felt that the news was not conveyed in the way they would have wished, the most common complaint was that there had been a delay in telling the mother, or that the husband or other family members were told before the mother. Another dissatisfaction was that the person who informed them seemed impersonal, and avoided talking to them afterwards.

When the news is broken to the parents and later, it is vital that there is communication between the parents and their doctor or other professional staff. There are so many questions which arise and so many feelings to be conveyed, that the parents need the time and private space to be listened to and to understand their experiences.

6. Autopsy

An autopsy had been performed in 60% of the deaths. Most women who agreed to an autopsy said they were glad it had been done. Only two women regretted not having an autopsy done. The cause of death was reported to have been discussed with 82% of the women in the study and most of the women were satisfied with the explanation.

One of the most insistent questions in the parents' minds is 'Why did my baby die?' Unfortunately, doctors may not know the cause until an autopsy has been done. If you are unsure of the cause of death, you may request an autopsy. Usually it will take four to six weeks before all the tests and results are complete. Your doctor will receive the results and an appointment is made with him to discuss the findings. An autopsy does not always provide exact answers, but it often rules out particular causes which may be of greatest concern.

7. Hospital experiences viewed as least helpful to the bereaved mother

In order to have a clear understanding of helpful experiences, it is important to be aware of the opposite end of the spectrum, i.e. those experiences found not to be helpful. So the women in the study were asked to list hospital experiences which they felt were least helpful in their grief. Some mentioned instances of lack of sympathy from staff and times when staff seemed impersonal. If a staff member appeared not to acknowledge the death of the baby, the mother saw that as a lack of sensitivity. There were reported instances of inappropriate comments and advice, such as 'Don't cry, or you'll upset the other mothers'. Lack of information about their baby's condition was resented, as was absence of advice about their own grief reactions. Receiving information in an inappropriate place was seen as insensitive. One couple was informed of their baby's death in a public part of the hospital. Being in a postnatal ward surrounded by other members with their healthy babies was not seen as helpful; nor was the lack of facilities for a partner to stay overnight.

8. Hospital experiences viewed as most helpful to the bereaved mother

Mothers reported that they were helped by staff members who showed empathy and compassion. They were grateful for encouragement to express their feelings. Where appropriate, they appreciated being involved as much as possible in their baby's care and to be with and to hold their dying or dead baby. They also appreciated receiving accurate, up-to-date information regarding the medical aspects of their baby's condition. Generally, they found it helpful to receive information from the staff regarding the grieving process and being reassured that their reactions were normal. Doctors or other involved staff members spending time with them so they could express themselves and ask questions was remembered with great appreciation. Generally the mothers preferred to have a private room with overnight accommodation available for their husbands or partners.

Summary

Some of the experiences women have found helpful to them in resolving their grief are as follows:
- Seeing and holding the baby.
- Naming the baby.
- Bathing and dressing the baby.
- Having photographs of the baby.
- Having the hospital bracelet, cot card, lock of hair, footprints, blanket or other remembrances of their baby.
- Having family members and close friends to the hospital to see the baby.
- Being involved in funeral arrangements.
- Attending the funeral.
- Having the opportunity to talk with staff members who were empathic and understanding.
- Receiving information on the grieving process.
- Having accommodation for their partner to stay overnight with them.
- Having an autopsy on the baby and later discussion with their doctor as to the cause of death.

What can hospitals do to assist bereaved parents?

The women in this study have given clear and consistent reports of experiences which supported them in their grief. They have also conveyed hurtful or negative experiences. This information can provide guidelines to hospitals for developing effective policies to assist bereaved parents. The insights offered by these women were supplemented by the experience of innovative programmes observed in England, Canada and the U.S.A.*

One of the essential starting points in developing adequate support programmes is the acknowledgement by the hospital administration that the needs of bereaved parents are unique and require consideration by senior members of staff. While in-depth discussion and consideration of this issue may provide the cement to form a foundation, the foundation itself is in the clear policy statement developed by the hospital. Many hospitals do not have such a policy, or if they do, it is a perfunctory one which addresses specific legal obligations of the hospital, such as autopsy forms, death certification and burial procedures. Very often the emotional, psychological and support requirements of parents are left to the discretion and goodwill of individual staff members. This is more than adequate if parents have a caring and understanding obstetrician and/or paediatrician, social worker and nurses who listen to their needs, support and guide them in understanding their grief reactions. However, the opposite situation may also occur. The welfare of the parents can be a matter of random chance or luck which is not adequate.

When a hospital is prepared to put down in writing a policy on the care of bereaved parents, it is a clear statement of concern and commitment. The policy itself will inevitably encompass a broad range of issues, which may include:

- procedures for staff to assist bereaved parents.
- nursing care plans for the assessment of a woman's needs and appropriate support required.
- educational programmes for all hospital staff to increase their ability to support the bereaved parents.
- provision of a multi-disciplinary perinatal bereavement team to give specialised care to bereaved parents as well as support for direct-care staff.

* Special acknowledgement is given to the Perinatal Bereavement Team of the Women's College Hospital, in Toronto, Canada, whose innovative programme of services for bereaved parents provides an inspirational model.

- information booklets for parents, to assist them in understanding their grief reactions, how to deal with funeral arrangements, how to assist their surviving children to cope with their grief and where to turn for help if they need it.
- a 'Quiet Room' specifically for the use of bereaved parents.
- follow-up care for the bereaved mother. Hospital liaison with community health nurses who would be trained in bereavement counselling and provide support to the mother over the first difficult year.

While it seems an enormous task for hospitals to embark upon, there has been an increased awareness in our community of the major effects on women's mental and physical health following the death of their baby.

The provision of the best possible services for bereaved parents in hospital is real preventative medicine. If we can help the mother and father to a healthy grief reaction, we can prevent future marital and family disharmony and future health problems. So the real target is to support the psycho- logical health of families at a very formative and vulnerable period.

Clearly, the ultimate power to enhance the quality of care for bereaved parents lies in the hands of the hospital. However, it is important for bereaved parents to know what services are useful and what can be provided so that they, individually and collectively, can influence hospitals, by making them more aware of their needs as bereaved parents and providing feedback on the quality of the care they have received.

I hold her in my heart

The good, the bad and the beautiful is the most apt description for the life and times of Tansy, our fourth beautiful daughter, who died on the fourth short, painful day after her birth. Every attempt to convey the myriad of feelings and thoughts surrounding the past two-and-a-half years falls so far short of adequacy, I am attempted to abandon the task right here. But in the hope that changes are only ever possible by greater knowledge and understanding of life's taboo areas I shall make my small contribution. Also, for myself, in each re-telling, each lot of tears, there maybe comes a little healing.

It is the suddenness, the randomness, that is the most shocking—birth and death together. It is just not supposed to be this way. How hopelessly we are prepared. My first thoughts are that my little one suffers no more; there is some relief that the struggle is over, reason enough for a small measure of gratitude. But we just as quickly seem to realise we are left to face the grief, an initial overwhelming, unbearable emptiness, which we must now acknowledge, however reluctantly.

Here we are, trying to cope with that event, we as parents have all sometimes thought about, however fleetingly—the prospect of losing one of our own children in our time. Well, it's as bad as I'd imagined and worse. We are chosen, not haplessly I believe, but nonetheless, whether we like it or not. As we cradle our little girl in our arms, her newly-dead little body still warm and sweet with that special baby smell, I am struck by the incongruity of the clothing the staff have chosen to dress her in. How ridiculous, I think to myself; there is little need for the pretensions of clothing. A blanket would have sufficed. In fact, I am quite hostile about this and subsequently complain to the hospital that this procedure robbed us of precious moments after Tansy died. What a pity they didn't ask us. We loved her in nakedness in life so why not in death! Could clothing somehow make her more acceptable? Well, certainly not to us.

In Perth's major maternity hospital, where babies probably die daily, we sit in a tiny little coffee room adjacent to the special nursery, waiting for them to bring us our daughter. Incidentally, we must fend off other parents trying

103

to take a break from their vigils. We come to think later, that this is the value they place on dying—sandwiched in this silly room, trying to take it all in, all those special moments that will be the sweetness of Tansy's time. Absolute numbness and shock are setting in, yet there is a vague recognition that our lives are already inexorably changed. Only time will ever give us any shape and substance to what is happening. For the moment, no matter how incongruous and indifferent the setting, we must grasp the little left of Tansy's existence with us. There is futility as I rock and cradle my baby, knowing I could not do this for her in life and that it now only helps me in her death. Yet I breathe in that sweetness, stroke her and love her just the same as we now must instantly accept that this is all there is to be. I don't like this at all but acceptance must be quickly learned and the most made of every moment, albeit with constant interruptions.

Still the whole thing seems vaguely surreal as, like a little doll, I place her in the hospital basket, kiss and pat her, tuck her in as I did all my other girls before. Yes, Tansy reminds me exactly of my dolls and childhood in her lifelessness, as we leave to go home to the rest of the family for what has now become Christmas Eve. I sense the institution has little to offer. We'd be better off at home, even if I think I'd rather be dead, too.

I am carried on only by thoughts that she is not suffering. I am completely empty, lost in nothingness, not in need of the tranquillisers and sleeping pills being instantly proffered, no doubt as some sort of salving of the medical consciences forced to bear witness to this misery.

By God it hurts, but I will not be doped; of this I am quite positive. These events will be burned into our psyches in the most painful way but at least not blurred and distorted, or worse still forgotten in the half haze of drug zombiedom. We've come to find that many things done supposedly with the good of ourselves in mind are in fact more likely done to protect and ease the pain of those around us. In the weeks that follow, some friends flee. We face the abandonment of the bereaved and it seems that we are to be doubly punished for failing.

And gossip. Many seem curious but lack the courage to actually ask us what is really happening so what they do not know, they invent. All more pain. All never forgotten, although some day we will try to forgive. There are tears, pain, anger, recrimination, more pain, self-pity, rage. Everything that ever happened played through our minds and replayed again. Yet always a vague hope that some day this will all make some sense—that there is some meaning and that this sadness will not detract from our lives as it does now—a feeling that we will survive, no matter what.

Born seven weeks early after an easy, straightforward, natural labour, Tansy developed hyaline membrane disease—not initially a cause for great concern, but the degree to which she subsequently developed it was rare. The hospital told us she was the first child of such advanced gestation and otherwise good condition to die of such complications in five years. But when did statistics ever matter to a mother, when it was her child they were talking of?

Therein maybe lies the reason we feel the system failed us. The death of a baby who otherwise seemed to have such good prospects did not seem to be as readily tolerated by her medical attendants as we would have hoped. Doctors are not God. We learned death is not always well handled even in a place where it happens as frequently as every day. For death involves spirituality and an overall philosophy to life and living. It requires courage in the face of natural fears; strength when weakness would be easier. And doctors and nurses are not necessarily any different to the rest of us. We know this now. They tried to console us with statistics, but it seems these matter more to scientists than mothers! How much I wanted to hear just one of them say, 'We're sorry' We certainly would not have thought any less of them. Instead, most of them chose to pull their medical cloak more tightly around them. A chance lost to share in a little healing.

They told us Tansy had only a one-in-ten chance of survival twelve hours after she was born, but somehow we just knew she would be that one who pulled through. Dying was for other people's babies. Somehow hope survived right until her life was over. Even after being removed from the ventilator, my first words as they brought her into us were 'Is she still alive?' Yes, hope really does spring eternal. The first words that tumbled from the sister's mouth as she handed Tansy to us, together with the photograph of our newly dead daughter, were: 'You may want an autopsy': I mentally recoiled. Unfortunately, it is hard to forget some things.

Much of the sadness that persists to this day relates to why it was not possible for us to be with our little girl as she died. Like lambs to the slaughter, we did as we were asked and left the nursery, as they promised us they'd bring her straight out to us. In the fifteen or so minutes we waited, I even imagined some miracle was happening and life and health were being restored to our baby girl, Could miracles happen this Christmas? Today we can only hope that another sort of miracle is happening and that parents such as us are not excluded and denied the opportunity to participate in our children's most difficult moments of transition from life to death. It has been hard for me to get over feelings that, as a mother, I let Tansy down by not being with her. I have still to make my peace with this.

Maybe it was in deference to the feelings of those who had tried to help us, that we did as we were told and waited outside in the coffee room. Certainly, had we been thinking clearly, we would have stayed. Although we had resisted all staff exhortations to have some rest, take a break or whatever, we had steadfastly and without question maintained our cotside care of Tansy, attending to the few chores they allowed us, like dabbing her mouth and eyes with water, as the atmosphere dried out her little body. We stayed, not because we believed she would die but because we knew she was ill and needed all the care and support we could give. This seemed to amaze some of the nursery staff and we felt our presence was not always appreciated by some who choose to run these places for the convenience of the institution. But, as it was our baby's only home on this earth, we stayed anyhow and we were grateful for our fortitude later. By standing our ground then, we are left less often with thoughts of 'if only', something I have come to hear a lot from other bereaved parents. I reconcile myself most times with thoughts that we did our best to make the most of what there was and do what we could and there is no doubt we are not often plagued with thoughts that we,or anyone else could have done more. This has been important in the healing process. Also to learn to forgive—not easy, but we try, realising that we are far from perfect ourselves.

However, even two-and-a-half years later, there are those moments recalling the horror of it all that I actually will try to reject the notion and in fact find myself wondering did it actually happen. Was it our family, did we indeed have a beautiful little dark-haired, dark-eyed, fourth daughter?

A brief respite in our minds as we still try to cope with what happened. But there is the little pink tag, the dress she wore that I'd hoped to bring her home in, the Scottish shawl we lovingly wrapped her in for the funeral service and the tiny foot- and handprints. Yes, yes, she did exist. From May to December she was very real as she rocked and rolled around in my tummy, when she put out her tiny fingers to grasp ours when we first saw her in the humidicrib, blinking her gorgeous little kitten eyes in the bright lights of the special nursery.

Indeed bitter grief could never ruin the sweetness of her time. Tansy has left us a legacy of infinite value. She has added a great dimension to our lives and our great sorrow is that we had so little opportunity to add to hers, to show her the world we enjoy. But every day I send her my love. I hold her in my heart, I think of her, love her and share memories of her with the children. Brendan and the circle of fiends, very many of them drawn to us in Tansy's dying, with special gifts of love and support then which makes for much deeper and meaningful friendships now, and a greater family bond between us all. These were Tansy's gifts and make her a very special member of our family. She will always have a place that is her very own—one that can never be diminished by time or other people's (well-meaning!!) attempts to obliterate her from our lives.

Recently we had our fifth child and firstborn son, Jack. He did not replace Tansy in any way, as some others seemed to have hoped—maybe still not having comprehended that children are not somehow interchangeable! But he is a gentle reminder to us all that life goes on. It is bittersweet for all of us. Through suffering we hopefully keep growing, find more in ourselves, more to give and experience. None of us has a chance to go back, nor would we wish to, and I guess it is about here we somehow find ourselves. Accepting what is, just as it is, trying to keep uppermost the good memories—acknowledging the reality of the bad, while not allowing ourselves to become their prisoners.

I think most of all Tansy has really been about accepting ourselves. I can only love and thank Tansy for her special part in our lives.

'How fleeting are the joys we dote upon,
Like apparitions seen and gone
But those who soonest take their flight
Are those most exquisite and strong,
Like angels' visits, short and bright,
Mortality's too weak to bear them long.'

J. Norris

October 1988

Today I wish to add a thought, as it nears the fourth anniversary of our daughter's birth. Little did I think then, that I would be holding yet another beautiful daughter, Primrose, born to us just two weeks ago, on September 30th. It has not been easy. There is much to remind us of little Tansy . . . a dark thatch of hair, more kitten eyes, long slim fingers which uncurl to grasp our own. But at the same time there is hope. Hope of a new future encompassing all of the past, together with a growing strength that has come a lot, I feel, from surviving these past four years. I am sure I did not believe I could ever feel as joyous as I do at this moment, with five beautiful healthy children and a family that has grown stronger in the face of tragedy. Tansy is a little light in all our lives, who helps to remind us of what it means to be a real family—loving and caring for each other. She is with us all forever and it has been through her presence in our lives that we have come to know the fullness of Shakespeare's words: 'Love doth indeed not know its own depth until the moment of separation'. We hope we all radiate a little more of this love. If this be so, then our lives are inexorably for the better for Tansy's coming.

Primrose's name means 'little first one'. So they may think this a strange choice for a fifth-born daughter, but for myself, I think of her as the first daughter born to parents very changed by the life and death of their very special fourth daughter. Nothing will ever bring her back to us physically, but in many ways she has not left us, as she continues to play her special part in this, her family. God bless Tansy.

Chapter 5

Grieving together separately

You have thought
About these things
That can be thought about
But never discussed.

Yet with another,
Hand in hand,
May we not wonder,
And come to understand.

Ainslie Meares

When we first submitted our research paper to the *Medical Journal of Australia*, one of the editorial comments was 'What about the father's grief? Why didn't you include fathers in your study?' The answer is that interviewing 110 women and analysing the results was an enormous project in itself. To make a beginning, the mother's grief seemed to me to be the foundation stone, and the logical first step to be taken. However, it is extremely important that we understand the grief of fathers and surviving children as well as the effects on the marriage and the whole family system.

This chapter is written from the accounts of bereaved fathers. These men have shared their own journey of grief and their individual ways of coping.

There is no doubt that the father is greatly bereaved after the death of his baby. However, his grief may differ from his partner's in its intensity, duration and expression. Perhaps it is this difference in the grief pattern which is the hardest for couples to cope with. Why, at a time of their greatest sorrow and vulnerability, are they not able to feel, react and respond in harmony? Although it may not seem so at the time, each may be providing the balance for the other and for the family as a whole. Then again, it may be that we are all so unique in our grief process that to have two individuals grieving in the same way at the same time is almost impossible. Whatever the reasons, it is clear that the lack of synchronisation which often occurs can be quite distressing to each of the partners.

A woman who loses a baby faces multiple losses which stem from the deep bond which begins prior to or from conception onwards. Because of the inherent differences in prenatal attachment to the baby, the father may not experience the depth or pervasiveness of the wound felt by the mother. It is very dependent on how closely bonded the father felt to the baby prior to birth, or how much contact he had with the baby after birth. So for both physical and psychological reasons, the father's grief may be less intense and of a shorter time span than the mother's. Needless to say, this does not mean that the death of this baby was not a great loss to the father. Nor does it mean that he is a less sensitive or feeling person. He really just had less time than the mother to form a connection with the infant.

One of the greatest difficulties faced by men in their grieving is the expectation placed upon them by society. Men are seen and expected to be the strong protector of the family. In addition, particularly in Australian culture, men are not supposed to express feelings, particularly those of sadness, sorrow and helplessness. Crying is often considered a sign of weakness. Thus, a man can be placed in the unenviable position of feeling bereft and powerless, while trying to provide strength and support to his wife and children.

Many fathers tell of friends and family asking how the mother is feeling, if she is recovering and if there is anything they can do to help her. Yet rarely do they acknowledge that the father too is grieving and in need of emotional support. It is as if people see the father as the 'keeper of the gates', standing between his wife and the outside world, allowing what is needed to come in and keeping out anyone or anything which may add to her pain. It is helpful if those close to the couple can acknowledge the father's grief, even if it is not as accessible or demonstrative as the mother's. The father too needs someone to talk to, someone to listen and someone he trusts with whom he can let his emotional guard down and express his innermost feelings.

When both the mother and the father receive adequate support, they are much more able to support each other. Confusion and despair may ensue when there are different experiences of grief in the couple, with each believing that the other one just doesn't understand. It is so hard to find the words to reinstate communication in the marriage, when each person is at a different stage, or coping in a different external way. Often, for couples to simply understand that their grief is different and that each may not know how the other is feeling, can be the beginning of re-establishing their bond.

The majority of women in the study felt that the death of their babies produced greater closeness in their relationships with their partners. About one in five women said there had been no effects in their relationship. Approximately the same number said they felt there had been a detrimental effect on their marriage in that they felt more separate from their partners. The loss of a baby does have a major impact on the marital relationship and in some cases the marital bond can be shattered. With most couples, though, the relationship is cemented and enhanced.

Those near the couples need to understand that the differences in reactions are only differences and not indicators of a lack of love or caring. They need to provide support to the father and the mother based on individual needs. If friends and relatives can be open, honest and at ease with the couple, this will help comfort the whole family.

Reflections of a father

As a father and husband I found the loss of our baby girl Tansy devastating at the time and for some six months later. However, I found to my shock that not only did I endure the slow death and loss of Tansy but I was to endure my wife's enormous grief—grief I found to be much deeper than mine and the children's. Her loss annihilated her, crushed her spirit and her will to live at different times.

My wife's grief, due I think to her far greater bonding and contact with Tansy in the womb, created in me a feeling of helplessness. I was unable to feel as deeply in a natural way. I found it hard then to cope with my life and felt shattered that the loss of Tansy (in itself almost too much to bear) was to cause so much ongoing pain for myself, my wife and our children.

I don't think I could have handled the situation as I eventually have done, if I had not involved myself so closely with my wife at the birth and during the following three days. I experienced the full vigil over Tansy with Wiggi my wife, and although our three girls at home needed my time too, I think the time with my wife and critically ill baby helped me to understand the grief that was to come later.

Maybe one of the hardest things to grasp about infant death is that one is losing a human being. People around do not know the child and so the loss seems often to be exaggerated to an outsider. I am aware that I too could have been less affected by Tansy's loss if I had made less contact. The grief I felt for Tansy then became overpowered by the loss of normality in our home as we all grappled with her loss.

I am very aware that the number of family breakdowns after child loss is high and I hope continuously that the scars and hurt from those last two years can be overcome and left behind.

Tansy will not come back, but she has touched the hearts of many people, and given our family a bond of love and spirituality that otherwise may have never developed. Tansy reminded us all of the gift of life on earth.

A couple's shared grief: Sarah's mother

It was three years ago that Sarah was born and died, and her birthday has just passed. Again my husband and I (and this time our new daughter) took flowers to her grave. For the first time I was unable to even mention her name on her birthday to my mother. Now talking about her is hard and I would rather get on with the happy part of my life—the present. It is all right if I initiate the conversation, as then I am well braced, but if someone else brings it up I find my voice gets tight and I feel as though I am trembling inside.

This reaction is quite different from my first reaction after Sarah died. Initially I wanted to talk and talk and talk about her, to show everybody her photograph and to print her name indelibly on the world, to make her mark. I was proud of her. For a long time I felt I still had her and the sense of loss which everybody told us about seemed to have evaded me—something for which I felt rather guilty. Strangely, when my parents sold our family home just recently, the sense of loss I experienced then reached nightmarish proportions.

It seems that my first reaction was one of extreme shock which lasted some time. I experienced an hysterical attack after visiting a friend with a new baby and was admitted to hospital. The symptoms included heart pain. Sarah died of a congenital heart abnormality. That happened eight months after her death. I also experienced two very early miscarriages—a sign of stress.

After a long time of intense, almost convulsive anger and a period of counselling to help us cope with a new pregnancy, I conceived again and now am a mother to another beautiful daughter. I find I am totally indulging myself in the experience. I dread weaning her and cannot leave her easily. I just want to be with her constantly, to sit at home with her and lap her up. I have an irrational fear of any medical treatment she might need.

Looking back over the events I realise that what helped me to cope was above all my husband and the intense closeness I felt towards him through it all. He was always there. Had he not been there I really feel I would have fallen apart. It was this closeness and intimacy that was a positive aspect in a series of incredible knockbacks. First the diagnosis, then the weekend of horror in the neonatal unit when I longed to nurse and comfort my baby and see an end to her suffering, but couldn't. I was only told by nursing staff who were too busy to be caring that she was awake when, oh God, I just wanted her to be asleep and out of her suffering. It was then that the knocks came one after another until I was numb. We were expected to sit and watch our beautiful and, as we had thought, healthy baby, who had brought us such unspeakable joy for a whole week, be turned into living death, dependent on a life-support machine. The idea that she suffered haunted me above everything and I desperately wanted people to tell me that she didn't. Fortunately with modern medicine pain was probably fairly well non-existent, but in her little mind, did she have terrible hallucinations, awful sensations? Was she missing the warm care of her mother? These questions still haunt me and I have to comfort myself with the fact that the drugs sedated her enough to alleviate it all. But did they?

When she died it was an enormous relief. She no longer suffered and would never suffer again. Thank God.

Strangely, little things worried me. The fact that the lights weren't ever turned off in the unit; Sarah hardly experienced the dark. Nor did she experience the warmth of the sun, nor nature. However, she did experience the rain on her face when she was being transferred to the children's hospital. That was important for me—something she knew away from the artificial, clinical world.

Her funeral I wanted to be just between my husband and myself, but so as not to hurt other family members they had to be included and that became a focus for my anger. They didn't understand; they intruded on my strongest means of support, the intense intimacy with my husband. We were burying something of our relationship, not of anybody else's. Of course, Sarah was theirs too, but it was hard to be rational.

Afterwards, my milk dried up virtually straight away, from the shock, but the other signs of having given birth were constant reminders; the bleeding and excess weight. I felt I had a desperate need to scream and scream, to squeeze out all that grief, but somehow it was all locked inside.

We had just bought a new house to accommodate a family and the move was another positive in our lives. We redecorated a bedroom and I did it for Sarah deep down. It was obviously for a little girl, but we daren't make it too obviously a baby's room.

I went through a period of wanting to be nowhere but home, just to bury myself in my nest, safe and cosy. I couldn't bear the idea of going back to work as that was obviously saying I am here again because my baby has died. It felt regressive, so I did a course instead. New course, new friends and a new home, all seemed to help.

Some friends I lost, others I gained. Little comments people made went deep and some finished a friendship, others made one One woman in particular seemed very intrusive with all her help. It was not until later that I really appreciated all she had done. We talked endlessly about it all and her concern showed that my baby was important to her. She had allowed Sarah her place in the word. Like the joy of that first week, it was something gained, not lost and on Sarah's first birthday she gave me a potplant with a pure white flower. It now flowers each year on her birthday. This woman is now probably my best friend.

A couple's shared grief: Sarah's father

Yesterday, for the first time (I think), I felt real anger. I was reading a newspaper article reporting on an experiment in the U.K. which deliberately focused on neonates, testing the comparative effect of different levels of anaesthesia during open-heart surgery. How could they operate so callously? Isn't it axiomatic, a first priority, that something as helpless as a newborn baby must be protected from pain and the cover should never be lifted if there is any suspicion of suffering? I was choking with rage and simultaneously weeping, and I realised that it was a delayed reaction to something I had been deliberately suppressing. The trigger, I think, was the reference to curare, used as a paralysing drug. For me that was the most shocking aspect of Sarah's death, when they brought her back from surgery a broken little body covered in tubes, her arms and legs in that awful cruciform position. She did seem crucified, and she stayed that way for two days, immobile, as the condition deteriorated. We could only believe what we were told and hope that there was no pain.

At that stage my only perceived emotion was a passionate wish that she should die quickly and be spared a life of impairment and suffering. I know now that there is an intense anger against the individuals and the medical system which perpetrated such butchery, and I don't think that I shall ever be able to think with equanimity about major surgery.

At the time my feelings were dully fatalistic. When the condition was first diagnosed, I wanted to run away, hide and be with my thoughts. But I had to stay with my wife and see it through with her and of course I could never leave Sarah. The events unfolded with a ghastly inevitability. I lost hope prematurely when I first saw her in a humidicrib. Rather irrationally, but, as it turned out, appropriately, the humidicrib had come to symbolise death for me, and nothing that ensued was a surprise. The only thing that was unexpected was the sheer horror of it all.

One of the worst aspects at the time was the repeated necessity to sign agreements authorising major operations, and that for an infant who had no concept of what was happening to her. It seemed to place in my hands the decision whether she would live or die, be mutilated or stay whole. In fact I had no choice. We were offered hope; the odds were dangerous but not unfavourable, and I could not deny my daughter the chance of life and ultimate happiness. In retrospect I wish desperately that I had refused it all, so that she could have passed away without the trauma of surgical intervention. But how was that possible? I would have blamed myself for her death, and indeed I would have been responsible for it. That saves me from any real feeling of guilt, but I have a deep frustration still, overwhelming sadness and a feeling of explosive anger which I understand, but cannot neutralise.

What helped me? Little at the time, I think. The fatalism took over, and I seemed to experience the affair through a filter of emotional numbness. Even when we held our dying baby, after the paraphernalia of life support had at last been disconnected, beautiful experience though it was, it did not immediately arouse my emotions; it was a calm valedictory, shared with my wife. The total sharing of suffering was primarily important. It resolved some of the immediate trauma and prevented obsessional onesidedness.

I never felt isolated in my emotions, as had tended to be the case before. Caring for somebody else whom one loved and empathised with also helped avoid being immersed in self-pity. In a strange way too my atheism helped me. I could accept that what happened to Sarah was a random genetic flaw, highly unlikely to recur and just one more imperfection in an imperfect world. I don't think that I could have endured the discipline of reconciling the event with belief in an omniscient, benevolent deity, and my lack of belief did give some comfort.

Since the tragedy I have discussed it regularly with my wife. She feels things more immediately and tends to initiate the subject. I react to her emotions, which are often a catalyst for my own. There are all sorts of events, predictable and unforeseen, which trigger emotion. Visits to the grave are a certain way of tapping a deep well of grief, but there are also unpleasant random shocks like the newspaper report of the neonatal experimentation. All this evokes emotion, primarily of grief but latterly of anger, which I would otherwise half-consciously suppress. Friends do not help directly. I'm afraid that I don't wear my heart on my sleeve, and they tend to respect the privacy of my emotions. It makes life and work more immediately comfortable, but it doesn't help the grieving process.

Counselling has been important from time to time, mainly to cope with secondary problems which were becoming intractable because the unresolved grief at Sarah's death left so little space for other things. The emotional impact of the affair isn't surprising. What I was unable to realise, though, was the depth and tenacity of my feelings and the efficiency of my subconscious mechanisms for blocking them. I now know why I was consistently unhappy and agitated even when everything was superficially good.

Having another, quite beautiful, daughter is a comfort but no consolation. She is a unique little personality, and in no way can I see her (even if I wished to do so) as a replacement for Sarah. My love for her very often evokes the sense of loss for Sarah, which I shall probably always feel. If anything, it makes the relationship deeper and more rewarding, for the immediate joy in her has the counterpoint of the underlying grief for Sarah. The two emotions seem in a way symbiotic; the one sharpens the other. I suppose that the trauma of loss eventually becomes part of the fabric of life. It is always there and deepens one's perceptions while adding a tinge of sadness to everything.

Chapter 6

How children cope with the death of a sibling

Death

When someone dies it hearts so much. When Tansie my baby sifter died it was very sad for all of us it was frustraiting and confuessing. Tansie died because her lungs weren't working—When Mum and Dad told me it was Chrismas Day I felt very sand and I didn't talk for ages. I still haven't got over it because it was very sad. I love her very much and wish she could come back but I know that's not possible. In my dreams and when I am in class and upset I think about my little friend Tansie.

> I send
>   her all
>   My Love.
>   Pippa.

Tansy

Tansy was born on the 21st December 1984 and died three days later on Christmas Eve.

Tansy was my little sister who had everything to live for and it was very annoying and sad when she died. Tansy was born on a Friday night when my aunty came over for Christmas. I was sleeping on the couch when Dad came home from the hospital and told me that I now had a third little sister. I was really pleased and went back to sleep. Next morning we went down to the hospital. Tansy was in the Intensive Care room at King Edward. Pippa, Cassia and I put on white gowns and went into the room. For an early Christmas present I gave Tansy a little pink bear which was put into her humicrib. I touched Tansy's hand gently for a second or two. We visited Tansy a few times before she died. On Monday I came home from my friends and Dad told me that Tansy had died. Christmas that year was sad and a happy day for most people, but not for us. Christmas was very hard to enjoy and you just have to put on a brave smile even if your not happy. We had a funeral at home and Tansy was cremated. Her ashes are under an angel in the house. We all loved Tansy and it was so unfair that she died. I know that Heaven is supposed to be a happy place so Tansy should like it there. I hope she does. If Tansy's happy I'm happy.

Emma.

When a baby dies, the parents are often so shocked and emotionally overloaded that even making simple decisions can be draining. Yet, when there are surviving siblings, the parents must, in addition to dealing with their own grief, do what they can to assist their other children to deal with the death in the healthiest possible way.

Usually, the automatic reaction of the parents is to try to protect their children from the pain of loss and grief. They may send the children to friends or relatives, or be very calm and strong in front of the children so they don't see the parents' distress. While these actions are based on caring, the parents, by taking them, may unknowingly be hindering the children's own grief process. As much as possible, children need to be involved fully with their loss; to be encouraged to see the baby and to attend the funeral or any other family ritual. In this way they are able to comprehend the death of their sibling and they also learn through their involvement shared with their parents, that death and grief are a natural part of life.

Even if one tries to protect children from grief, they will pick it up, for they readily absorb the feelings and reactions of parents, without a word being said. Excluding children may only build walls between them and the parents and may also set up a model for the children of withholding emotions and giving them the impression that death and grief are fearful and secret subjects. The ongoing involvement of the children is beneficial to their own grieving process and in preparing them for handling future losses. When children are included fully in the grief of the family they often become a great source of comfort to the parents themselves.

Children's grief reactions

Of the women in this study who had surviving children, about half felt there had been some negative effects on their children. These effects included observable distress, emergence of feelings of insecurity and sometimes, changes in behaviour.

When children lose a sibling they experience many losses. Firstly, they have lost a brother or sister who may have been quite special to them and secondly they sustain a loss of security or trust in life—sometimes expressed as a loss of trust in their parents, doctors or hospitals. From a child's point of view, parents and doctors are often seen as omnipotent and should have been able to save their little brother or sister. Thirdly, they may feel the temporary loss of the normal intensity and constancy of their parents' love and attention. Finally, they may notice the loss of the usual emotional stability in the family and may try many ways to make things better. Therefore it is not surprising to see some adverse effects on their behaviour and stage of development, following the death of a sibling. In most cases, what mothers meant by negative effects were mainly normal grief reactions. They saw that their children were sad, angry or withdrawn and that they often seemed to cling more to the mother. They also showed signs of taking steps backwards in some aspects of their development. Again, this is not unusual. We all, even as adults, regress to childhood ways of soothing ourselves in times of crisis and when we are bereft.

The women in this study were also asked whether they felt closer, the same, or less close, to their surviving and subsequent children, since the death of their baby. The majority felt closer to their children and only three of the 110 felt less close. However, over 60% of the women said that the death of their baby had made them more anxious about the safety and health of their surviving and subsequent children. Twelve of the women said that they decided against having any more children because they feared a repetition of the tragedy. Both the clinging response of the surviving children and the anxiety felt by mothers about their safety and well-being are opposite sides of the same coin. When any of us loses someone we love, it is almost inevitable that we will fear for the welfare of those close to us.

The reaction of a child to the death will depend on many factors such as their previous experiences of death, their own unique personality and their social, cultural and religious background. The age of the child will also influence the level of understanding and way of coping with the death. A wide range of responses is normal, from incessantly talking about the sibling and death to not speaking of the loss at all and behaving as if nothing has happened. The following are typical reactions of children to grief, based on their different stages of development.

The pre-school child

It can be most difficult to explain death to young children. Pre-schoolers tend to view death as temporary because the concept of 'permanent' is not yet comprehended. Often, they are unable to accept the finality of death and can only associate it with a sleep or journey from which one returns. If death is explained to them in terms of having gone to sleep, they may take this literally and become anxious about falling asleep for fear they may die as well. With children in this age group it is often best to explain the death in terms of the natural order of life; a simple indication that the baby will not come back is often sufficient. Seeing the baby and attending the funeral can help them understand more clearly.

Little children may not seem to be grieving. Parents may think 'they didn't take any notice, they just kept playing'. In these circumstances parents should try to understand that to a child, play is a natural way of expression. Just as adults 'talk out' feelings and problems, play is a child's work.

Dealing with complex feelings and concepts such as death can be a difficult task for a young child. They may deal with the problem piece by piece over a long time in their questions, dreams and play. It is very important that they set the pace for the parents to follow. Listen to them, try to understand their expressions through their play and answer their questions simply and honestly.

Often the child's response to the death is similar to that of the parents, because children are so attuned to the emotional life of the family. In fact the child often expresses what the mother really feels. Sometimes, the child may put all of his or her energy into taking care of and nurturing the mother, for fear of losing her too. However, the child will not always react to the loss as the parents do. It depends on the meaning the new baby had for that individual child. The child may say what seem to be quite uncaring things, like 'Why don't you go back to the hospital and get another baby!' In order to assist the young child, it is vital that the parents try to see through the child's eyes and respond at that child's own level of understanding.

Children aged six to ten years

Children in this age group have begun to realise that death is final. While they comprehend that all living things do die, they still don't view death as something personal. They have difficulty in understanding that anyone they love could die. Children of this age may have unexpressed fears of their own death. If the parents become withdrawn, anxious or over-protective, the child may interpret these as messages that the world is a very dangerous place and worry that parents may not be able to provide protection. These feelings may cause the child temporarily to lose trust in its parents, itself and in life and become quite fearful. It should be conveyed to the child that although the baby died because of being very sick, no one else is in danger and healthy children do not die.

It is not uncommon for young children to attribute blame to themselves for anything that goes wrong in the family. In their 'magical thinking' they may feel anxiety and guilt that perhaps somehow they were the cause of the death. It is absolutely crucial that parents reassure children that no one could have caused or prevented the death by actions, thoughts or wishes. Young children believe that wishes are powerful and may think that somehow they caused the death, particularly if they personally were not looking forward to the arrival of a new baby. They need to understand clearly that no one is to blame, no one hurt the baby and most importantly, it was not their fault.

Children aged eleven and older

Children from the age of about eleven onward can think abstractly and have the ability to conceptualise death in an adult way. They are often more curious about the biological aspects of death. They understand the permanence of death but may need to grapple with questions of 'why?' Sometimes they may experience feelings of guilt or fear similar to that experienced by younger children, that they in some way were responsible for the death of the baby. Under these circumstances, the child will need support and reassurance. Around the age of fourteen onwards they may raise spiritual and psychological questions about death to try to crystallise their beliefs about the meaning of life.

Most of us, as adults, can allow ourselves to break down and regress in situations of intense emotion and react as a child. However, adolescents may not be able to do so, because often it is important to them to feel that their emotions are under control. Adolescents are dealing with so much emotional growth that they can become frightened that they may be overwhelmed with emotion. They particularly need the adult, parent model of being prepared to break down and express feelings. This parental example allows the adolescent to move into those intense feelings without so much fear and anxiety.

Guidelines to assist children with their grief

Children know intuitively how to grieve. If we really watched them we could learn a lot. Young children have the ability to express feelings freely, which is the most healing part of grief. They are much less capable of being brave, strong, nice or good just to make others feel all right. This is a barrier which adults must struggle to overcome. Children cry when they're sad and show anger when they're hurt. So, if grief is an emotional reaction to loss, then we can trust children to be experts on grief.

What children want most at a time of loss is the understanding of their parents and family. They can cope with grief and loss, if they are told the truth simply and honestly and are allowed to share with loved ones their natural feelings.

For many of us, confronting a child with the reality of death seems such a painful task. Our own fears of death and society's denial of death can make our approach to children difficult. Despite all this, children should know what has happened and parents' openness can provide an invaluable foundation stone for their children's present and future ability to deal with loss.

In being attuned to the feelings of our children, we can help them to understand themselves. Children need their parents to be aware of the nature of their feelings and the intensity of them. They want their parents to be able to put a name to their feelings and experiences and to convey that what they're feeling is understandable. If we can be open and honest with children, nothing else needs to be done except for us to learn from them.

Chapter 7

The journey of maternal grief

I believe:
Somewhere
Hidden within me
There is a key
That can unlock the doors
To greater understanding.

I listen for the whispers
That come from within.

But who can hear the whisper
'Mid the noise of trying?

As with the bird
On his lonely flight,
It's in the calm and the stillness
That we hear the whispers
Which tell us the way.

Ainslie Meares

Grieving is the normal emotional response to the death of a loved one. It is the space and time we give ourselves for the wounds to heal. We need time to grieve. Each person will grieve in his or her own way and the road from initial shock to final acceptance is a painful one. Although some of the experiences along the way can be anticipated, there is no map. Grief is a journey, not a task. It is not something we can work at very hard to complete: its completion relies on us allowing the process to unfold of its own accord. The memories of the loved person need to be brought alive.

The process of maternal grief involves the mother's relationship with her baby throughout pregnancy. The bond which the mother has formed with her baby is broken when the baby dies. In her grief, the mother re-experiences the bond, relives her hopes and dreams and gradually, over time, recovers. As her grief is resolved, her pain dissipates and the bond is reinstated. Her child remains special to her; a part of her self.

Although it is helpful to understand that there are stages to the grief process, they are not distinct and separate stepping stones. A mother's response to the loss of her child is as unique as her child. Her reactions to each of the problems she faces along the way need to be her own. No one experiences the stages of grief in the same way at the same time, or in the same order. Often the feelings will be interwoven.

The initial impact on a woman of the death of her child can be quite overwhelming. She may experience a sense of numbness throughout her body as well as emotional deadness. The mother may feel distant and detached with no apparent emotion; she may feel as if it is just too much to take in. The experience of shock is a natural protection to the bereaved mother, allowing her time to adapt to the reality of the death of her baby. At this time, it is very difficult for the woman's mind to comprehend even the most simple information or to make decisions of any kind. She may completely forget conversations with her doctor or other staff. It may not be until after the main shock has receded that she can think clearly, take in information and ask questions. She may feel bewildered and confused. This numbness may last for hours or weeks—allowing time for her to acknowledge the extent of her loss. .

Sometimes both parents experience a sense of chaos and lack of direction in their lives, over the weeks or months following the death of their baby. There may be an urge to make everything different. They may think of selling their house, moving to another place, or switching jobs, in an attempt to make things better. However, it is important that major decisions be left until there is some resolution to the grief.

When the anaesthetic of shock has worn off, bereaved mothers begin to feel the full range of their emotions. The emotional intensity and fluctuations can be quite painful. The bereaved mother needs the continued caring of her friends and family and she herself must ensure that she is well nurtured. She needs rest, healthy food and experiences which she personally finds relaxing and soothing. In every sense, it is a time of convalescence.

It is only natural to be angry after the loss of a child. The anger needs to be expressed, whether it is towards the hospital, staff, doctor, husband, family or friends. The bereaved mother needs someone to listen to her and understand the reasons and the intensity of her anger. All too often, however, the anger experienced after the death of a baby gets turned inward, and the feeling of guilt becomes the main focus for the mother. As one woman explained, 'I was seized with feelings of guilt. I went over and over in my mind: was there something I did to cause my baby's death? What went wrong? Was it the day I cleaned the kitchen, or the day I walked so far to the shops in the heat?' There is such an overwhelming need to answer the question: Why did it happen? Yet often there is no satisfactory explanation.

The bereaved woman may also feel that she is a failure as a wife and mother. One mother said, 'I feel so bad about all the sadness I've caused my husband.' Another woman related that she hated her husband and felt he was to blame for her baby's death.

Since the death of a baby is so devastating for a woman, it is not surprising that she may have wide-ranging feelings of fear. When life has dealt such a severe blow, it is hard to trust again. She may have intense feelings of danger with a sense of urgency, or a need to take action. She may fear the deaths of other loved ones around her and become anxious over the health and well-being of her husband and other children. She may experience a generalised fear—an anticipation that something terrible will happen again, especially if she is to become pregnant again. As one mother said, 'I have flashes of feeling cold all over, just shaking with fear. Fear, fear, always fear. I have such a longing to be a mother and yet I'm so frightened.' At these times, the woman needs the reassurance and support of someone she trusts. She needs to talk about her fears and be listened to and understood.

The loneliness and sadness of a mother's grief is very common before she reaches a sense of resolution. Often, when family and friends consider that their support is no longer needed, that is the very time that the mother is facing the emptiness she feels inside. Life may seem to lose its meaning and colour; there is a flatness of emotion and interaction with the world. The bereaved mother now, more than ever, may feel alone, isolated and out of contact with her family. She may experience changes in her appetite, sleep disturbances and an inability to communicate her inner feelings. She may find it very difficult to break out of her isolation into previous activities. As one woman said, 'I feel so alone, so isolated. Everywhere I go there are pregnant women or mothers with young babies. I just can't go out for fear of meeting them. I just want to be left alone.'

Eventually the mother will sense that her intense journey of grief is coming to a close. She will slowly begin to stake her claim in life and look to the future. When she re-engages in activities in her world, and begins to make plans, she will realise that she is emerging from her cocoon of grief, a long and painful process; her bond with her lost child forming again as her attachment to life is restored.

Legacies of our daughters

When I was twenty-five weeks pregnant, an ultrasound confirmed that I was carrying twins. At twenty-seven weeks, our beautiful daughters were born. From the start of their very short lives, the doctors were honest about their futures: they would do all they could, but it depended on how the girls coped with their prematurity. We were also very aware of the types of mental and physical handicaps they could have if they lived, and this introduced feelings of confusion and guilt, as well as the numbing shock we were experiencing. Confusion as to whether we wanted them to survive at all costs ('all costs' meaning to us: the girls' quality of life; the effects on our marriage; and the effects on our thirteen-month-old daughter)—or whether it would be kinder (but not easier) to allow them to die without adding trauma to what they were already facing. Out of this confusion came the guilt. Were we wishing away their lives, while there was still some hope for their survival?

We were never faced with that decision. When they were two days old, they died within four hours of each other.

When I reflect on the ways my husband and I grieved, I think we made it harder on ourselves by not admitting that things were not all right. I didn't want friends, relatives or even my doctor to recognise that I wasn't coping with the grief that was overwhelming me, so I 'put on a brave face' for the world . . . inside I felt as if I had been shattered into millions of pieces and I wasn't sure how I'd put these pieces back together again.

The only thing I held onto was that if losing the babies caused all the pain, another baby would take the pain away. My husband didn't want another child at that time; he didn't want to take the risk of more pain, but I wasn't capable of seeing things from his point of view, and I applied constant and harsh pressure to him, until I was pregnant. This pregnancy added more stress at a time of still intense grieving for us. Throughout this pregnancy my doctor gave me openings to discuss how I was coping, but my standard reply to any queries was 'I'm fine'. I felt as if my husband was ignoring the pregnancy; a defensive reaction in case this baby died too, and I felt that he was avoiding me by working long hours and weekends. I think he did this because it was only at home that I could express my emotion and cry and admit that I wasn't really coping. He couldn't cope with my grief as well as his own. During this period I spent many hours either cuddling my daughter and crying, or having long showers while I cried. I also found I cried a lot while driving or doing mundane household tasks.

Our son was born fourteen months after the twins had died. The magical cure I was hoping for did not manifest. I found for the first few days after his birth, I could not relate to him because he wasn't the girls. I did a lot of grieving in hospital and found the hospital staff and my doctor all concerned and willing to sit and give me time to talk things through. Even at this time, I would not allow anyone close to me to know that everything wasn't wonderful.

It was around this time I finally admitted that the stumbling block in my grief was guilt. I felt guilty that I had not protected our girls from a premature birth and I blamed myself for not recognising that I was in labour earlier than I did and perhaps have gone to hospital earlier and maybe with the use of drugs, held off their birth. It still took nearly another year before I had the courage to approach my doctor with these feelings and discuss them. It was only after talking this out that I was able to deal with it and work through grief and arrive at a positive outlook for the future.

I often wonder if I had not tried so hard to cope, if I had admitted that it was too much for me, and sought counselling or allowed friends and relatives to help, whether I could have faced and dealt with my problems in less than the two years it took.

The only place I showed some of my feelings was at the support meeting of SANDS, and it was at these meetings that I felt confident in letting some of my guards slip, because I knew that none of the other bereaved mothers there would judge me or would dismiss me as a hopeless case. It was through the encouragement of the group that I finally returned to my doctor to discuss the guilt feelings I had. I found it important to talk with other bereaved mothers because they understood that grief doesn't disappear after a few weeks, which seemed to be the time some people expected one to grieve for. It was also reassuring to see the various stages of grief, stages of 'getting better' and to know that although it wasn't going to be easy, one did 'get better'.

It is now four years since the death of our girls. I have talked and talked about that experience through SANDS, until it sits comfortably with me. Tears will still well in my eyes if I dwell on that period but that doesn't happen often now. If I'm asked, I can talk about it without crying. It is something that happened, it was and still is, the saddest period of my life, but I have worked through the pain and now concentrate on our two beautiful, healthy children.

My husband didn't talk about his feelings during his grieving time. For him it was an intensely private grief that he couldn't share. He still finds that to talk about that period is difficult and so, unless I initiate the topic, he doesn't bring it up. One of the many things I have learnt from this experience is that people don't grieve in the same way at the same times. One must never judge people using one's own experiences as the baseline. Everyone must be allowed to work through grief in his or her own time and way. Early on, I couldn't accept my husband having a different grief pattern from me, but I discovered how unrealistic and unfair it was for me to expect him to grieve my way. Although we don't discuss what happened much, having shared that experience with each other and survived, it has given us a special, deeper aspect to our relationship—one of the positive legacies our daughters gave to us.

Chapter 8

The lonely hours:
who will understand?

> To give one's self over
> To the other,
> Utterly
> We learn something
> Of that other giving-over
> Which transcends it all.
>
> *Ainslie Meares*

'After I got home, I found the saddest aspect was that people only want to listen for so long and then you have to keep things bottled up inside you. With a baby who lives such a short time, and doesn't even come home, it is hard to grasp the tangibility of that birth and the death. You are left feeling empty and robbed, but somehow not believing it happened—hoping it will come right sometime. I got no cards or anything to say that my son ever existed, which makes it harder.'

This was taken from a letter written by a recently bereaved mother. It conveys perfectly the feelings bereaved women often feel when they return home.

The reality is that women do feel devastated, empty and robbed. Yet friends and relatives believe they will be their old happy selves within a week or so. After a perinatal death, it is often assumed that the mother will recover quietly and quickly, with minimal trauma to herself or her family. This is the myth that women face in our community.

It is vital that bereaved mothers do have the support of their close circle of family and friends for them to resolve their grief. The bereaved mother cannot make this major transformation in isolation. Her thoughts and feelings must be shared. She needs someone close to her to mirror her experiences. Otherwise, her very real inner life can become distorted and devalued through the denial of her reality.

Women in this study were asked to comment on their perception of the supportiveness of those around them. The majority said that their husband had been of some support to them, while the remainder described their husbands as angry and uncommunicative. Only ten of the women reported that their family and friends had been supportive and the others did not feel they received the support they needed from family and friends.

Since adults mainly experience intense grief only when they have had a long-standing relationship with the person who has died, friends and relatives of a bereaved mother often find it difficult to understand and empathise with her grief over a baby whom they may never have seen. They may then offer what seems to be consolation, along the lines of 'Don't upset yourself, you can always have another one', which the bereaved mother sees as a devaluation or denial of her reality.

A most significant finding in this study was that the intensity and duration of a woman's grief was not related to the gestational age of the baby, whether the baby was stillborn or died at a very early age, or how long the baby lived. Women's reactions were not dependent on whether they had had many previous losses of children, or if this was their first experience of losing a baby. These results echo the feelings conveyed by women in therapy. To a bereaved mother this particular child was special, just as in families where there have been no losses, a mother sees each of her children as unique.

This is why bereaved mothers find it so terribly painful, when those around them suggest that this child is a nonevent and easily replaceable. However, comments from those close to the mother are made with good intentions, in that they desperately want to help and are lost themselves for words or ways to relieve the mother's pain. They may not know she needs to express the pain of her grief in order for it to dissipate. There is no easy way to grieve.

The emotional support which may normally be available to the bereaved from family and friends may be greatly reduced or even absent. Sometimes mothers need to be told that the support they should rightfully be receiving is truly absent, and is not a figment of their imagination.

In speaking to bereaved mothers or their families, it is useful to consider, by comparison, the support a widow would receive. If a woman had recently lost her husband and she did not have the opportunity to see him after he died nor be involved in the funeral arrangements, or attend the funeral, she might sense a lack of reality in his death. Furthermore, if after the funeral she then received no cards, flowers, or consistent involvement and support by her family, she would find it difficult to deal with her grief. If her family and friends then began to avoid speaking of her husband or his death, and when she showed her tears or sorrow they said 'Now don't get upset, you can always find another husband', it would be devastating for her. How could she cope?

If a bereaved mother's family and friends respond to her as they would do if she had lost a very close adult loved one, then they will be providing the support she needs. For a bereaved mother's grief is as intense and real as if she had lost her husband, and those who love her need to acknowledge and reflect the depth of her grief. Women should not have to withdraw and isolate themselves in order to properly grieve for their loss.

The majority of women involved in this study reached a healthy resolution to their grief and did not suffer long-term physical, psychological or social disturbances. It was these women who had support in the reality of their grief from someone close to them—either their husband, or friend, or family member. It only takes one person for the mother to feel understood. Most grief therapy happens within the family or close social network.

Where do women turn if they don't have the support they need, or the experiences to help them grieve? It is important for bereaved women to speak to someone they trust, someone they feel will listen and who knows and understands them. It may be that there are people around them like their husband, mother, sister, friend who have remained silent, believing this would be helpful. However, if the bereaved mother can explain to them that it is healthy and normal to talk about the death of her baby and to express her feelings, then their understanding may unfold. They need to know that expression of feelings and thoughts is never hurtful, it is only the silence that hurts.

If there is no one the mother can talk to in her own circle, then she has to reach out. Some of the many ways in which she can seek help include support groups, her doctor, community nurse, minister, social worker, clinical psychologist, psychiatrist or bereavement counsellor. Asking for grief counselling or therapy is not a sign of weakness or illness, but a sign of insight, courage and strength. Therapists who work in this area have great respect for those who reach out and express their needs. It should also be recognised that a particular support person may not necessarily suit everyone. It is not so much the academic credentials that signify an ability of a counsellor or therapist, but the understanding that the woman feels she is receiving.

In all cases the woman is free to make a choice of her counsellor or therapist. If she has seen the counsellor or therapist and does not feel there is an open, caring communication, she should seek other help. The feeling of being understood deeply is such that, when she finds the right person, there will be no doubt as to her choice. Many women find their main, or additional, support is talking with women who have travelled the same path and who understand the journey. Support groups such as SANDS provide a safe, caring environment, where bereaved mothers have the space to express themselves and to be heard. Alternatively, members of support groups are usually available to talk with the mother individually.

Bereaved mothers tell us that their loss and their grief are real. We must take time to acknowledge their feelings and experiences and we must show sensitivity and compassion in all our interactions with them. Above all else, a bereaved mother needs to have someone to trust with her most intimate feelings of grief. It is in the trusting relationship that she can feel understood. The understanding will enable her to reinstate her trust in herself and in life.

The arrival of a grandchild

Sometime in our lives we face the tragedy of the death of a loved one. It is particularly sad when it is the death of a baby.

In my case, my daughter announced she was expecting her second child and this brought a lot of joy to our family and her friends. The arrival of a new baby is a great event to look forward to. Time goes so quickly and the expected birth was not far off and I came in to mind my three-year-old grandson.

With a knock on the door in the early hours of the morning we were naturally anticipating that a baby girl or boy had arrived safe and well. For me that joy was to turn to sorrow. To learn our grandson had arrived but was severely handicapped and might only have hours to live just left me devastated. My main thought was how can I help my dear daughter face this terrible unexpected news? Shortly after the birth our family doctor arrived to talk the situation over with myself and my eldest daughter, who had already been to the hospital. He was also very upset, it was for him the first delivery of a baby with 'spina bifida' and he was also at a loss to think he hadn't picked up any problem during the pregnancy.

The doctors at the children's hospital explained the options open to my daughter and her husband. Their decision was to let 'nature take its course'. From that time on I had to get myself together and care for a three-year-old, as I'm sure he was sensing something was wrong. My grandson John was taken home after two weeks and cared for very lovingly, as no one knew what his life span was to be. I went to the local library to see if there was anything written up about this very sad situation we had all been placed in. There was just no information available at all. The next step was how do we help? It was hard to comprehend that in the 1980's there was very little help available. The hospital had a nursing sister for home visits, daily if required, but her programme was full and her visits could only be short.

Our baby lived five weeks, he was certainly loved, but then the situation was to get no better. How did we help these young parents cope with their loss? Their young son was going thought a hard period also; he wasn't included in all the trauma taking place and I know now it is vital for other children to have things explained to them. There is no reason why children should not see a baby after death, for to a small child I think it would seem to them that their baby had just gone to sleep.

Then the time came for our daughter and son-in-law to face the fact that after nine months of waiting, their baby died. It is hard for family and friends to know how to help. Do we talk about the baby's death or do we talk about other things? I'm sure I could never give the answer to this, as every person has their own thoughts and emotions and it is hard to express how you feel. Society has not been trained to handle traumatic experiences openly; we have to bottle our emotions within ourselves. This should not be the case—we should all be able to handle such a tragedy.

From all this, I feel in the last three to four years SANDS has been a great help to my daughter and to myself, and to a lot of parents and their families. From my first meeting with SANDS I felt that finally my hidden feelings came out in the open. I think the more we can all talk about our own feelings about death, the more comfortable we feel inside, particularly with the case of a baby. That 'baby' was a person and even though he may not have been with us for long he was still a person. I needed to talk about him, there were lots of nice things to remember about him.

Going back many years I knew of several girls who had a stillborn baby, yet the subject was never discussed, or even mentioned. My neighbour was expecting her first child and he was stillborn, but no one ever said anything. This was particularly hard for me as I was then expecting my first baby. They were to be only a month apart in age. I felt very uncomfortable walking past her house with my healthy baby girl and she didn't ask for months if she could see my baby. My neighbour did have two more healthy boys. Yet thirty years afterwards, this woman had a nervous breakdown, which was brought on by her going back over the first birth. She started to ask questions. What happened to her baby? Was there a grave? Was he christened? Her husband had the unenviable task of trying to piece it all together with her. In those days, the death of a stillborn baby was left in the hands of the hospital and there was no involvement of the parents, so there were no memories to even begin to put together. So there was nothing for her to hold on to and make sense of.

These memories came back as I struggled to understand how to help my daughter. Who does a mother turn to for comfort? Maybe it is easier to talk to someone outside of the family circle. Are friends the ones, but then again they could give the impression, 'Oh well, you had a baby, it died, you get on with life', others may not be interested in how the mother feels. Sometimes you just feel helpless. This is where I think it all comes back to a group like SANDS. This is where we got the help we needed.

I remember at a SANDS meeting, a young girl came up to me and asked what my interest in SANDS was and I explained to her I had lost a grandchild. I guess she was curious why an elderly grey-haired lady was at a SANDS meeting. She started to cry and I asked her if she had lost a baby. She said she had, but it wasn't full-term. She said her husband had shut the whole thing out of their lives. She had no family or friends who she could talk to. She had just spoken to her doctor and found out what happened to her baby's body and was very upset. She said she wished so much that the hospital had told her she could have had a funeral and burial. Even though she didn't have the money for one, she said she would have found it somehow.

So here we all were at a SANDS meeting, all with different stories, different experiences, different needs. But there was a common bond we shared and that seemed to make all the difference. Sometimes I think back thirty years ago when my neighbour lost her baby and how much silence surrounded her. I realise a lot of progress has been made in helping parents after the death of a baby. I think particularly having SANDS to turn to has been important for myself, my daughter and so many other families. Yet I can also see there is still much to be done.

Chapter 9

Relatives and friends:
how to help

Tenderness
Is a feeling
That comes for a moment,
Then persists in memory
Forever after.

Ainslie Meares

The support a woman receives from her family and friends does affect how she copes with her grief after the loss of her baby. If she has a supportive family and social network she is most likely to be able to resolve her grief in a healthy way. If she does not receive the emotional support she needs at this time, her recovery is greatly impeded and she may develop quite serious health problems.

In having to deal with her pain on her own, she becomes more and more isolated and withdrawn. If all her emotional energy is being used just to function and deal with the loss, sooner or later she is unable to give to anyone else. Thus a vicious cycle begins. Friends and relatives hold back or avoid the mother because they feel uncomfortable, then she, feeling unsupported, turns inwards and eventually those close to her feel she has changed so much they cannot contact her and she cannot reach out. Bereaved women in this situation experience enormous losses. It is as if the woman has not only lost her beloved child, but has emotionally lost her husband or family or friends because they are out of contact. The sense of being lost is very painful.

The issues are complex and there are many effects of feeling unsupported. If the mother continues her journey of grief alone, she begins to lose her self-esteem and confidence in herself. She may be less able to nurture her other children and as a result, lose the enjoyment and confidence she previously had as a mother. The children may then become more demanding and she may feel even more pressure and may blame herself for not being able to cope, or not being a good enough mother. The rewarding relationships in her life may be greatly reduced and whereas she once felt secure and confident as a wife, mother and friend, she may now feel depressed and inadequate.

There are two statements which are essential to understanding the experience of bereaved mothers. Firstly, loss is real. Secondly, to feel understood is essential to resolving the grief. The death of a baby leaves the mother hurt and wounded. If someone close to her provides the love, caring and understanding she needs, then the wound begins to heal. However, if the support and understanding is minimal or absent, the wound actually deepens. Although it is most helpful for women to receive support from several people close to her, it is enough if just one person really understands her. This chapter is written in the hope that friends or relatives of bereaved parents will understand that they themselves could make all the difference, and that they would be helping not only the mother's health and well-being, but the health of the family as a whole.

How can I help? What can I do?

Paradoxically the answers to both questions are at once both remarkably complex and simple. The complexity lies in our belief system and in our own fears and anxieties about death. It may be that to really help a bereaved mother, we first have to look at why it is so difficult just to be with her and why it is easier either to avoid her, or to talk superficially about other topics.

The following beliefs are often quoted by family or friends and seem to stand like mountains between these 'helpers' and the bereaved:

- 'It was only a baby you didn't know, so don't get upset.'
- 'You can always have another baby.'
- 'Crying only makes it worse.'
- 'If you keep busy you will get your mind off the baby and be happy.'
- 'You should be grateful for the children you've got.'
- 'It is a blessing the baby died' or 'It was God's will.'

Comments such as these, which are not unusual for a mother to hear after the death of her baby, tend to foster isolation, by denying the real experience of the bereaved woman. These beliefs, expressed as platitudes, do not have a neutral effect. They actually are very hurtful, and can make the feelings worse.

There is no doubt that it is extremely difficult for someone who has not lost a baby to be able to understand what it is like for the mother. The idea of birth and death occurring at the same time is so painful to accept that the mother's friends try to rationalise it, so that they too don't feel the enormity of the pain, or the unfairness of life. If we are to be really there for the mother, we have to look at our beliefs and the attitudes behind them. Yet, it is not enough just to avoid the platitudes. Even if the words are not said, the feeling is still being expressed and while this is so, the mountain will be there between them both, making real communication impossible. The myths must be addressed and dispelled before there can be a reaching out.

The other aspect that makes it difficult for someone to be supportive to the mother is the reality of death. In our society death is usually a taboo subject. Our focus is on youth, life and living. Most people never think of their own death or mortality except when someone they know dies. Usually they prefer to avoid the issue as much as possible. Faced with the death of a loved one, we probably think of our own death as well, which can be an uncomfortable and painful process in itself. When dealing with all these inner feelings it is hard to be responsive to the needs and feelings of the bereaved mother. While there is no magic way to dispel these fears and beliefs, if we are aware they are there and acknowledge them, then the mountain shrinks.

The third impediment to support for the mother is that often when friends and relatives genuinely want to help, they don't feel they know how to. They wish that somebody could tell them what to say and do, so they could do it. This is like the need for a prescription from a doctor to make us feel better. Bereaved people often ask, 'What should I do?' However, it is not possible to provide a simple answer to that question. Each woman is unique in her grieving and has different needs. Thus, to know what type of support a woman requires, we must listen to her very carefully.

When a woman who has lost a baby makes an appointment for counselling or therapy, it is reasonable to assume that she is in pain and that at least in some respect she is not receiving the support or understanding she needs. It is unhelpful to the woman to assume anything further, until she has told the story of her own journey. It is for this reason that the support of a bereaved mother is both complex and simple. The complexity lies in the need to drop one's own beliefs, assumptions and anxieties which stop us from simply being there with the mother as another person. The simple part is knowing that there is no right or wrong way to grieve and that all we need do is listen and try to understand. It is possible to have a general map of the territory and some signposts that signal that the woman is temporarily lost and in need of some direction, but generally all we need to do is follow her. The real expert on grief is the bereaved mother herself. When she listens to her inner voice, her intuition, as to what needs to be done, her path is clear and leads her home. The confusion and despair at feeling lost come when she hears others say that she's silly or wrong or crazy or unable to cope. Then she loses the trust in her own natural healing process. So, the task for helpers is really to hear and support her own inner feelings, without judgement, criticism or a need for her to be nice or good or happy.

It is important for counsellors and therapists of bereaved women to always be aware of the uniqueness of their grief, to look for the missing link in each woman's chain of support and direct her back to her own support system. The bereavement therapist, then, can fill the gap of some unmet need which ideally is a function of her family and friends. Together with the bereaved mother, the therapist can look at the map and see who and what she needs and how those needs can best be met. It is almost always a matter of communication. If the bereaved mother isn't initially understood, she will often decide to put on a brave face so as not to upset those she loves and thus she never talks of her pain or needs and those close to her support the silence.

If a woman does seek professional assistance, this does not necessarily mean that her family and friends are insensitive, or uncaring. It may be that the mother is confused and either does not know, or has difficulty in explaining in words, what she needs. Or she may feel that it is unfair to 'burden' her friends and family with her own needs and feelings. Sometimes in order to understand her needs, we must listen to what the mother is not saying, and this may be very difficult to do if one does not have training or an orientation to this type of attention. A counsellor or therapist can help the mother to better understand what she needs and assure her of the importance of receiving support from those close to her. She may then be able to explain to her family what she wants and perhaps be able to accept the support which is available to her.

It is important to know whether a bereaved mother has at least one person she can talk to openly. That is essential. It is also necessary to explore where her needs are not being met.

One woman needs someone to talk to, whereas another may need some time on her own just to walk and think. So it's really finding out how you can help. If you feel unsure what to say or do, the most courageous thing is to say 'I don't know what to say or do to help—but I want you to know I'm thinking of you, I care and I'm here when you need me.

It may be with you that she will feel comfortable to talk deeply. She may wish to tell her story over and over. Perhaps she has other children and what she needs most is for you to come in and take care of the children, or cook a meal, so she can have some space and time of her own. The most important thing is to be available and to be continually available.

In the interviews for the research study each woman was asked, 'If you had to comfort someone after the death of her baby, what would you do?'

- 'I would allow her to talk as much as possible and encourage her to remember as much as she could. I would talk of her baby as a reality and I'd use the baby's name. I wouldn't try to console her or make things better, as only she knows her grief and the depth of her sorrow.
- 'I'd just let her express her own feelings. If she wanted to talk—or if she didn't want to talk, I'd be there with her. I wouldn't give her any advice because I found that so annoying.'
- 'I would encourage her to talk and I'd try to show compassion and listen.'
- 'I'd sit and cry with her.'
- 'I would talk to her. Find out what she wanted and see if I could help.'
- 'Hold her.'
- 'Just let her know that if she needed me-I was there, but if she wanted to be alone that was OK too.'
- 'Let her know I'm there if she needs me and that it's OK to cry. I'd also try to help her understand it's a process and it won't always be as painful.'

- 'Assure her she's normal and not going crazy.'
- 'I'd encourage her family to be supportive.'
- 'I'd talk about her baby, about her experiences and memories of her baby. I'd talk about the baby as a real and special person.'

In essence the message is simple and clear: Be There — Be Available — Listen — Talk — Talk about the Baby — Express Feelings — Cry with her.

To be able to listen, to really listen, is the key to understanding and it is through understanding that the healing occurs. Often we think that listening is an easy thing to do, yet to listen deeply is sometimes difficult. It really means to listen with our heart and not our head. To be an active listener one needs to present back to the bereaved mother only what she has conveyed in words and in feelings. No other messages of the listener need to be added in terms of analysing or evaluating or judging. It is the true acceptance of the other person. When that acceptance is present, then the bereaved mother can grow and develop and move in the direction of psychological health. Such active listening is a very powerful experience for conveying the acceptance of the other person. It helps the bereaved mother find out exactly what she is feeling and by encouraging the expression of these often distressing feelings, she becomes free of them. The sharing of intense emotions makes them less overwhelming and more understandable.

Friends or relatives wishing to be truly supportive by listening and understanding may like to consider the following aspects of their own caring approach:

- Do I genuinely want to be helpful?
- Am I willing to accept the feelings of the bereaved mother?
- Do I really want to hear what she has to say?
- Can I spend time with her and support her emotionally?
- Will I trust the bereaved mother's capacity to deal with her feelings and to work through her grief?
- Can I appreciate that the feelings are transitory, no matter how intense they seem at present?

- Am I able to say when I don't understand or when I feel lost and confused?
- Am I able to remember that the bereaved mother knows what is best for her, and to trust that her responses are real and honest?
- Am I able to understand, without feeling wounded, and still make myself available to her, if she says that she does not want me around right now, but wants to be alone?

To support a bereaved mother, you need to be yourself, and to be open and honest with her. Then, she can be open and honest with herself and those close to her. Through this healing process her trust in life can be reinstated.

> When there's harmony
> There's nothing
> That need be said.
>
> *Ainslie Meares*

A family's story

The stories that follow have been kept together to form a whole. The parents, Carmel and Jim, showed in their stories not only different reflections of their grief, but also that they were in harmony and synchrony. The third account was written for Carmel by her sister, Maureen, on the first anniversary of her son's death. The letters were so deeply touching that they have been kept together and remain intact.

This family's story gave so many added dimensions to an understanding of how families and friends can provide the support and caring that is essential for a family faced with the tragedy of the death of a baby. Through Maureen's writing, we can also see the true impact that the death of a special baby can have on the whole network of extended family and friends. It also beautifully portrays the reactions of children and how each dealt with the loss of a brother; how well children naturally understand grief and contribute so much to the family in their own special way. Yet, most importantly, what these stories convey is that helping is not something we think about, but rather the response of an open heart. When we join together in this spirit of generosity as family and friends, everyone ends up being nourished and feels that sense of kinship and belonging that heals the wounded heart.

A mother's story—from Carmel

Anthony Matthew was born on Saturday 10th September 1983 at 4.00 p.m. He was our fourth child. His brothers were Gerard, 12; Damien, 2; and a sister Emily, 5. They came to visit Anthony on Sunday afternoon, and Gerard talked about teaching him football and cricket when he grew up. Emily was a little disappointed she didn't have a sister, but was happy she had a baby in her family.

Anthony's birth was the best yet, as I had an epidural anaesthetic, which for me was marvellous. He was a healthy baby and weighed 3.4 kg. He had his official check by the paediatrician at about midday on Monday, who pronounced him fit and well and couldn't foresee any problems with him. He congratulated me on a rather beautiful healthy baby.

On Monday afternoon I had trouble breast-feeding him and he would not stay awake, so with the staff's help and advice I tried to feed him boiled water. Sometime during the afternoon or early evening he started making little moaning sounds. I realise now it must have been the start of a very bad headache. Also during the afternoon the official photographer arrived to take photos, but he wouldn't open his eyes so she said she'd come back on Wednesday! I realised after Anthony died how unimportant it is for a baby's eyes to be open for a photo.

At the advice of the paediatrician, the staff put Anthony in a humidicrib as the evening progressed, and kept a close watch on him, and I went to bed very apprehensively about 11.30 p.m.

I was woken at 2.30 a.m. by the night supervisor and paediatrician to say not to worry, but Anthony was being transferred by ambulance to the children's hospital for tests, and could I please let them have a blood sample. It was like a nightmare coming out of a deep sleep to find that something was dramatically wrong with my baby. I rang Jim who was home with the children and somehow managed to get the message across that Anthony was ill, and he said he would come as soon as he could get someone to stay with the children. I went and watched in disbelief as the ambulance officers put Anthony, in the humidicrib, on a trolley and wheeled it out to the ambulance. Jim arrived looking like a ghost, and we went to the children's hospital.

When we arrived at the neonatal ward, Anthony was attached to all kinds of equipment and the paediatrician in charge told us tests had been done and he had strep B meningitis. He was on antibiotics and he had twenty-four hours to accept or reject the medication. We had a very sick little boy, but the doctor was very hopeful that he would pull through. The next twenty-four hours were a living nightmare. I stayed for most of it, but there wasn't a parents' room available so I rested occasionally on the lounge chair in the parents' coffee room and went back to the maternity hospital a couple of times to attend to medical necessities.

The neonatal staff were incredible with their devotion and caring for all the sick babies, and from memory there would have been about ten babies, a few on trolleys like Anthony, attached to all types of flashing and beeping lifesaving equipment. All our questions were answered about Anthony's condition. As the day progressed he seemed to have innumerable blood tests and was so tiny to have so many tubes running from his nose, arms, feet, tummy. He later had a tube attached to a vein in his head to take a special sample of Jim's blood—a new technique, tried for the first time that day, but to no avail. He appeared to be getting better a couple of times during the day but in the early hours of Wednesday morning the doctor broke the news which I had been expecting but dreading: 'You are not prolonging his life but prolonging his death'.

Anthony's kidneys had failed, he was probably blind and deaf, and was severely brain-damaged—if he had any function at all. He was in a deep coma and had been fitting for many hours (this wasn't noticeable because of the strong medication). I hadn't noticed, but his fontanelle was very swollen because of the fluid on his brain.

Mary, my sister, was at the hospital with us; she rang Dad, and the hospital rang our priest friend, Father Charles. They sat with us as we nursed Anthony as the equipment was turned off. The respirator was the last to go. I really believed Anthony would go on living and breathing, and that the doctor didn't really know what he was talking about. Anthony breathed for about one or two minutes on his own, and we nursed him as he was dying. I couldn't believe it when he stopped breathing, just a tiny beautiful little baby, so perfect and yet dead. As he died the staff dimmed all the ward lights. I didn't want to nurse him when he was dead and gave him to Jim, who didn't want to let him go.

It seemed like hours later we left—it must have been 4 o'clock in the morning—I do remember it was very cold. We went back to the maternity hospital and a bed had been made up for Jim in my room. I can't remember whether I slept or not, but my obstetrician came to see me and he couldn't believe Anthony was dead. We then had to ring a few friends and tell them Anthony was dead, then back to the children's hospital to see the paediatrician (what an incredible man; he worked the usual day and had come to the children's hospital in the early morning two days running) to discuss what we wished to do. Would we agree to a post-mortem? What a terrible decision to make. He explained the reasons why, but it was our decision. After much thought we said yes and have had no regrets.

What happened the rest of that day? It is very hazy. We went to Mary's and told Emily and Damien that Anthony was dead. Emily didn't really want to believe it. I wished she had seen Anthony after he had been taken to the children's hospital but thought she was too young and there wasn't enough time to make those decisions; he didn't live long enough, and I didn't really believe he would die. We then talked about a death notice in the paper. I felt like a robot going through functions that I had been programmed for, but was really not in touch with reality at all.

I went home from hospital next day as I couldn't stand the sound of babies crying. Even though it was a warm spring day, the house felt like a tomb, it was so cold and uninviting. We were expecting the undertaker. I rang my sister Maureen, who had arrived from Melbourne the night before, and said please come over. She helped me find some clothes for Anthony to be buried in; what a horrific decision to make.

Next day Gerard arrived home from school camp so we went to pick him up with the news that Anthony was dead. Poor Gerard, after a week of fun with school friends and to have to face the prospect of his brother's funeral next day.

We had a beautiful church service and private burial for Anthony, and were staggered by the number of friends and acquaintances, some we hadn't seen for years, who hadn't met Anthony but who came to say goodbye to him and be with us. I remember lots of flowers and crying and hugging. Anthony's white coffin was so tiny. Jim and I put him between us on the way to the Guildford cemetery. We didn't want a hearse for him. We only had family and a few friends at his burial. I felt like I was at a picnic at the cemetery, it was a beautiful spring day and we were all carrying flowers. We had a basket of camellia and rose petals to sprinkle over Anthony's coffin. I was dreading the coffin actually going into the grave, but we left it on the side because the straps weren't there to lower the coffin. What a relief for me not to have Anthony in that big black hole. I didn't stop to consider that he was dead and in a dark coffin!!

The sympathy cards and letters started arriving, and came and came and came, in an unending deluge of mail. I didn't know so many cared. Emily made it her job to open the mail. The house was like a florist's shop, the flowers were magnificent, and each day Emily chose an arrangement to put in her room. The phone rang constantly and so many people came to visit us before and after Anthony's funeral Everybody was shocked at Anthony's death because on Tuesday we had announced in the paper 'To Carmel and Jim, a healthy baby boy, Anthony Matthew' and on Friday they saw a death notice, and notice of his funeral on Saturday.

Anthony only lived three-and-a-half days but he touched many people's lives in that time and many more after his death. We now have another beautiful boy, Luke, but there will always be that gap in our family where he should be. We still leave his photo out for everyone to see and the children quite often explain to their visiting friends that he was their brother Anthony, who was very sick when he was a baby and died. Children cope with seeing his photo much better than adults who didn't know us at the time. But he was for a short time a living member of our family and will always have a special place in our hearts. Many people forget the nine months leading up to the birth of a baby. Anthony was very special to us from the time of his conception; I didn't only know him for three-and-a-half days, I knew him for three-and-a-half days plus nine months.

Special memories

Barbara, who worked at the children's hospital, coming to spend some time with us, just watching and willing Anthony to live. Her husband, John, coming in to spend time with Jim when he was attached to the blood separating machine.

My sister, Mary, caring for our two younger children. The priest who came to be with us and Anthony.

Anthony's Baptism. I didn't really believe he would die but the doctor suggested that if we wished, we could have him baptised. All I remember is a white tablecloth, and a burning candle, and thinking this is stupid, we'll have him baptised in a couple of weeks' time in our own Parish, with all our family and friends with us.

To know that our many friends and acquaintances were praying that Anthony would live when he first became ill. Father John coming and having tea with me at the maternity hospital the night after Anthony died. My dad being with us when Anthony died.

Later, friends and family ringing up to see if I was OK, and asking me to visit, and listening to me tell my story of Anthony over and over again. I was lucky to have some good ears to listen to me.

A father's story—from Jim: our beautiful baby

I have always felt I have had a happy life, although my father died when I was eleven and Mum had to scrape to make ends meet. But when Anthony died I felt an empty, gloomy, hopeless sadness, that I had never felt before.

I was with Carmel when each of our children was born, and apart from feeling I was in the way, I was always apprehensive during labour, knowing how many things could go wrong, and then silly with excitement when they were born and Carmel was well. The same for Anthony, even more so, because we realised he was probably our last child.

I had visited Carmel the day after Anthony was born with Gerard, Emily and Damien and we had all nursed him briefly.

All I could see was part of his face, but as I had a cough I didn't want to breathe over him for too long. The paediatrician checked him later and told us he was a fine healthy baby.

Late that night, about 2 a.m. the phone rang and Carmel told me that Anthony had been taken to Princess Margaret Hospital for Children. I remember thinking and saying it must be just a minor problem, but when Carmel cried and said 'He's so little' I felt the first real worry, and hurried to get our neighbour to look after Damien and Emily so I could go to the hospital. When we arrived at the children's hospital I was shocked to see Anthony in a humidicrib with so many tubes. The doctor saw us and explained Anthony's condition. I knew he was quite ill but could see he was getting the best care and felt almost relieved.

I don't remember much about the day. I remember sitting next to Anthony the next night, when Carmel had gone to have a sleep. He looked so strong and healthy even then; he had a beautiful stocky body and I felt that he was going to be fine. I was willing him to get well, and the longer he went just breathing steadily the more confident I felt.

Then about midnight the doctor attending told me what I could already see—that he was having convulsions and deteriorating quickly. I woke Carmel; she was out like a light and hardly able to wake. We had to face the fact that he was past recovery and that we would have to decide when to remove the life support systems.

I couldn't believe he wouldn't live—our beautiful baby. We had Carmel's dad, her sister Mary, our priest with us when the machines finally stopped and we could nurse Anthony. I sat nursing him for about twenty minutes, and would have stayed for hours if I could have. I found the hardest thing to do was to let Anthony go. I visited the children's hospital the next day with Carmel's sister to see his body, and again at the funeral parlour, where I took a teddy bear to put in his coffin. He was burnt at Guildford cemetery among the trees and bushland.

The Mass and funeral were more helpful than hurtful. We had picked the readings and so many friends came to be with us, and Carmel's sister Maureen stayed with us for a few weeks and was fantastic. I had two weeks off work, and didn't feel like going back at all. We spent a lot of time talking with friends, a lot crying, some laughing, like when we were leaving the cemetery and Carmel and I were left behind and had to come home with our parish priest.

Emily and Damien used to just come close and hold us when we cried, and they seemed to accept better than we could that Anthony had been part of our family and had died. They often ask to visit his grave when we are driving past, and I sometimes call in on my way home from work. For a long time I felt that I couldn't care much about anything, then I had a few outbursts of anger. Gradually we settled back into some routine.

We were amazed at the number of people who told us of children they had lost, or miscarriages. Some of them were friends we'd known for a long time and they had never talked about their loss before.

Now we have another baby, Luke. I have never thought of him as replacing Anthony, but he has brought back a lot of happiness.

I am more appreciative of our children now, and watch them growing up more carefully than I used to, and I am grateful to many friends who were close when we needed them. John, who sat with me when I was giving blood for Anthony, and he and our priest who prayed for Anthony to get well. I just cried then, because I realised we might lose him and it seemed so wasteful, when he was born so well.

Two friends with whom we had always been quite close saddened us by not contacting us and it was months later before we heard from them at all. They may have had their own reasons, but we felt hurt all the same.

I feel I have accepted Anthony's death now and moved on. But it has had a dramatic effect in ways I probably don't fully understand. I certainly don't worry as much about other things now, and enjoy life even more than I used to, but in a calmer way; I cannot describe exactly how I feel about Anthony, except that there seems a small area of emptiness sometimes when I see his photo, or think of him if he were growing up. The photos were so valuable to us; I can't imagine what it would be like to have none.

An aunt's story—from Maureen

ANTHONY MATTHEW SMITH
Born 10.9.1983
Died 14.9.1983

Dear Carmel and Jim,
How do I begin to tell a story of a little baby I never met? It is difficult to write as my mind seems unable to find the appropriate words I need. If I was a journalist it would be so easy. This is my gift to you on what should be Anthony's first birthday, but sadly it is the first anniversary of his death ...

Birth

To Carmel and Jim on Saturday 10th September 1983 at 4.00 p.m. a Son, Anthony Matthew Smith. Brother to Gerard, Emily and Damien. Both well.

What joy and excitement and such a relief. Our worries are all over and Carmel had the best delivery of all. 'That's it', she said on the phone when I rang from Melbourne to say Congratulations. Jim was ecstatic when I spoke to him, 'He's a little ripper'. Another boy and a mate for Damien. Anthony was introduced to his sister and brothers the next day. Gerard said he would teach Anthony how to play cricket and football. We all presumed Damien would teach him how to break the car headlights with a hammer.

Never a dull day in the Smith household. It had taken many years to get this family together. Anthony seemed to be a bonus.

On Monday Gerard went off to a school camp, miles away in the bush, to a station. Jim was minding Emily and Damien and all the extended family were thrilled that we had another grandson, nephew and cousin.

Death

The phone is ringing — ignore it — I must be dreaming — it doesn't stop — wake — get up — stumble through the dark to the kitchen — fumble for the phone —Time on the kitchen clock 3.40 a.m. Melbourne time. Is this a crank call? No, it's a person-to-person to Mrs Maureen Beetram. Yes, that's me.

'Hold the line', someone says. 'This is Princess Margaret Hospital, there is a call for you.' My knees go to jelly, my legs begin to tremble, and I slowly sink to the floor. Something must be dreadfully wrong — it's 1.40 a.m. Perth time and the dream slowly turns into a nightmare. Mary is trying to speak and she is obviously crying. She is trying to tell me something that I don't want to hear. It can't be true, 'Anthony is dying, I didn't want to ring you because I kept thinking he would get better, but he won't, and he is dying now.' The lump in my throat is nearly choking me, the tears are burning my eyes, and I remember saying 'Maybe a miracle will happen'. Then Mary told me that he is dying as we speak. Slowly it sinks in, this unbelievable news. Our special Anthony, born on Saturday, well on Sunday, admitted to the Children's Hospital on Monday at midnight with meningitis. Mary's voice seems to ramble on through a for and I hear her say words like, 'Meningitis, brain damage, kidney failure, maybe blindness, deafness'.

Carmel and Jim have been with Anthony for twenty-four hours and Dad is at the hospital with them and Mary. They have sat with him willing him to live, watching modern technology of lifesaving equipment keeping him alive. He has had a special transfusion of Jim's blood and it seems that it was unsuccessful and the antibiotics just haven't worked. Why Carmel and Jim's baby, why? why? why? The paediatrician has told them, 'You are not prolonging Anthony's life, but you are prolonging his death'.

After discussions with the paediatrician, Carmel and Jim decided that if Anthony was meant to live he would breathe on his own. With sympathetic support from the medical and nursing staff in the neonatal unit they asked that all the tubes be removed from Anthony's body.

Anthony was baptised by Father Joe, and Father Charles had also been to see Carmel and Jim while they sat with Anthony.

Jim asked the staff to take another photo of Anthony when all the tubes had been removed, and Anthony died in Jim's arms at 1.30 a.m. on Wednesday 14th September, 1983.

I think Anthony was already dead when Mary phoned me, but maybe she just couldn't tell me.

Jim took Carmel back to the maternity hospital, where the nuns had set up a bed for him in her room. It was probably only the beginning of their bad dream.

Me

As I sat on the kitchen floor in the dark after Mary's phone call, I knew I had to go to Perth. Many years ago when I left Perth I made the decision not to return for funerals, but this seemed different. My sense of isolation was overwhelming and Perth could have been on another planet. Bob just couldn't believe that Anthony could be dead.

Bob left for work at 6 a.m. and at 6.15 am. I rang Princess Margaret Hospital. I could barely speak, but I suppose the operators at children's hospitals learn to cope with telephone calls such as mine. I will never know the name of the Sister in the nursery who answered my call but she was wonderful. She told me the story of Anthony's last twenty-four hours, and that it seemed that nothing could have saved him. I tried to thank her, put down the phone and a sea of tears fell out of my head. I knew that I had to be with you and for the first time since the girls were born, I knew they had to fend for themselves, because I wouldn't be around. Sleep was impossible, and I started to pack my things.

I was still crying, when I rang Judy at 8 a.m. to tell her about Anthony. Jude and I have shared many laughs together and also many tears and I could only refer to her as 'my Melbourne sister'. She was shocked at the news, as only a couple of days before we had been talking about 'Anthony Matthew Smith', and you know that she has a Matthew. I told her that I wanted to go to Perth 'As I felt so alone' Mary-Louise looked at me in amazement and said, 'Mum you aren't alone, we're here with you.' I tried to explain what I meant but it was impossible. Judy offered to mind the girls during the day, and Bob could collect them at night. I knew they would be happy with Judy and they would have to cope without me. Bob rang from work to say that he had booked a seat on the flight to Perth at 6.45 p.m., arriving in Perth at 9 p.m. Perth time. I phoned Mary to ask her to organise someone to collect me at the airport. Bob arrived home at lunchtime as he had been at work since 6 a.m., trying to finish as much as possible so he could have a couple of days off.

I spent most of the day crying and Katie and Mary-Louise tried to understand . . . I kept thinking that we should be there with you, sharing our first family death, but that was impossible. All my friends were very supportive and very, very sad, and I'm sure that we were all thinking, 'It could have been me'.

Deborah, Mary-Louise's kindegarten teacher, offered to drive me to the airport, and she collected me at 5.30. When I said goodbye to Bob and the girls, I didn't even feel sad, I think I was just numb. I knew they just had to 'get along without me'. I was relieved that Bob knew how to care for them and that they wouldn't starve, as he was a better cook than me!

Deborah explained to the hostess that I was very anxious about the flight due to the circumstances, and when I got on to the plane, I was shaking so badly that she suggested a 'stiff whiskey' I nearly threw up just at the thought (of whiskey).

Anthony's Farewell

It is Saturday 17th September, 1983, a beautiful sunny day with blue sky and kookaburras singing in the trees while I hang out the washing. I thought to myself that Anthony would never hear the kookaburras sing.

Carmel is sweeping the sand off the bricks, and Jim is tidying up around the sandpit, and Emily's music is blaring through the house. How calm we all were.

Gerard and I went to the church with Joan, Michael and the boys. I remember talking about crying, and said 'If Gerard feels like crying, you guys stand with him but don't try to stop him, it's OK to cry and maybe we all will'.

Then what a shock. I couldn't believe all those cars parked outside the church were for Anthony's Mass and thought that there must be something else on in the church hall. But they were all there for Carmel, Jim and Anthony.

The church was crowded with family and friends, maybe 300 people, all to farewell Anthony Matthew Smith. Mary McGinnis played the guitar and her beautiful voice filled the church. As people listened to the words of the hymns some openly wept, and many tears were shed that day for Carmel and Jim. Father John, a quiet, retiring, shy man, found it difficult to speak, and we knew that he too was hurting inside. He said he didn't know why Anthony only lived for three days but told us 'Anthony's mission is accomplished' It seemed that every person in the church went to Communion; it seemed to take forever. Standing in silent file, I'm sure that they all glanced at Anthony's tiny white coffin as they passed.

Uncle Brian sat behind us and at one stage held my hand and then placed it on Carmel's shoulder. After Mass Carmel and Jim were surrounded by friends outside the Church, hugging kissing and just holding them. People stood in a queue waiting to speak to Carmel and Jim, probably not knowing what to say, but doing it so well. Maybe most of them were thinking: 'It could have been me, it could have been us'.

Carmel and Jim didn't want a hearse for Anthony's coffin and decided that they would take him with them to the cemetery. They placed the coffin between them on the back seat and as they drove away, I remember thinking, 'they should be talking him home from hospital today'.

The house was filled with people when we returned from the cemetery. It was Open House and lunch was organised by friends and ladies from the church. Dad and Aunty Margaret were discussing the funeral during the following week and Aunty commented on the Brotherhood of the Church, but Dad said 'Sisterhood'. And that's really what it was. Casseroles and cakes arrived daily, and local women seem to have organised a roster and each evening a meal appeared. Dad said that he didn't hear much of the sermon but he did hear Father John say 'Anthony's mission is accomplished.' One day we were taking Damien for a walk and Dad said to me 'It's up to each and every one of us to see that Anthony's mission is accomplished'.

During the following weeks it became obvious to Carmel that she was to swap roles and become the 'listener'. A few of her friends had never come to terms with the death of their children. Maybe they had never been allowed to grieve and had bottled it up inside. So now she sat in the sun sharing Anthony's death with them and listening to their stories.

Carmel and Jim, I was unable to share Anthony's birth with you but I know that you will understand when I say I'm happy that I shared his death.

Death is the final act in the opera of life.

Guildford Cemetery

This small cemetery where Anthony is buried is surrounded by trees. The sun was shining and we could hear the birds singing. Carmel said she felt as if she was going on a picnic in the bush.

Jim and I carried Anthony's coffin to his final resting place. The family surrounded Carmel and Jim and seemed to be in a circle, holding Anthony's coffin or just touching it. The purple violets sent by Pam and Guy lay on top. As Father John said the burial prayers I was still asking myself WHY? WHY? WHY?

We had two baskets full of rose and camellia petals and all the family sprinkled a handful of petals onto the grave.

I suppose each of us said a silent farewell to Anthony as we read the inscription on his coffin ...

'OUR DARLING'
Such a short life but he had a profound effect
on so many of us.

Mary

Mary thrilled at Anthony's birth. Another nephew and cousin to her baby David. Now the joy has turned to sorrow waiting at the hospital with Carmel, Jim and Dad. Reluctant to phone me because she really thought that Anthony would live. Many thoughts flit through my mind ...

Mary caring for Emily and Damien. Worrying about Jim sleeping in. Would he really be asleep from exhaustion and grief, or would he feel deserted and alone? Should she intrude? Trying to imagine how she would be feeling 'If I was him'

Mary crying, saying 'Why wasn't it me'? I haven't waited twelve years to have a family. I'm only thirty. I've got ten more years, Why? Why? Why?????????

Mary trying to explain to Jessica that Anthony was dead, and Jessica's reply, 'He is a clever kid, he will crawl out of the ground.'

Mary organising casseroles etc., to be sent home when Carmel was discharged from hospital.

Trying to hide David from Jim.

Mary sitting in the Church at Anthony's funeral feeding David Would people think her cruel and insensitive? But Carmel and Jim wanted her there. They didn't know that Carmel had said to Mary, 'David is your baby, not ours. But he is part of our family and you must not hide him away.'

Damien

How should a little boy cope with Death?

Who knows how much Damien really understood, but he knew something had gone wrong and he was very angry.

Angry because he didn't have a baby. Angry because Carmel wouldn't go and get David from Mary. Angry because she wouldn't go and get another baby from the hospital.

One day as we were out driving we went past a hospital and he said 'You get dead in there.' How could I explain that hospitals are meant to be places of healing???

Emily

Emily made up a prayer for Anthony while she was sitting on the toilet. 'Dear Anthony, I hope when you are an angel you will fly into my room.' She accepted Anthony's death with a 'calmness' that I can't describe, and she assumed the role of helper. Helping Carmel and Jim open the numerous cards and letters that arrived each day. Helping me with the daily task of watering the flowers that seemed to fill the house. Beautiful, beautiful flowers that gave us all so much pleasure sent by family, friends and business acquaintances. Every day Emily chose a different arrangement of flowers to go to her room. She told me 'that people sent the flowers to make us happy because we all felt sad that Anthony died'.

Emily wanted to see Anthony's body so she went with Jim and I to the chapel. She lifted the embroidered veil that covered the open coffin and just looked at Anthony. She seemed to fully comprehend what death meant; she knew that Anthony would not open his eyes. A pink carnation lay on Anthony's chest and she said it was the same colour as the toy that Uncle Noel had given her the night before. She and Jim put the little footy boots and the teddy bear in the coffin with Anthony, and we said her special prayer together. Then she looked up at Jim and said. 'Let's go home Dad.'

On the morning of the funeral Emily chose the music. From the time she got out of bed the house seemed to be jumping to the sounds of every nursery rhyme record or tape that she possessed.

A few days after the funeral she asked me where Anthony was because she wanted to send him a letter. I explained that he had been buried at Guildford Cemetery. Not long after that I heard her telling Damien that 'Anthony is at Guilford Cemetery in his grave in the ground'.

Many months later Carmel told me in a letter that Emily had coped better than the rest of the family with Anthony's death.

A Letter to Gerard

Dear Gerard,

How sad we all felt for you to arrive home to be greeted with such tragic news. It is difficult to learn to speak of death, but I'm sure now that you will always be able to help your friends if and when they suffer a bereavement. Sometimes the most important thing is to just listen.

You knew Anthony for such a short time. Mum remembers you nursing Anthony on that Sunday and you told him that you would teach him how to play cricket and football. But that wasn't meant to be. So now you will have to concentrate on Damien.

Did you feel angry and cheated? It may have been easier if you had seen Anthony in the Children's Hospital with so many tubes attached to his little body trying to keep him alive. I don't think Mum or Dad could ever explain the pain and anguish they felt as they watched Anthony's little body fight for life. We were all pleased to have you home from the school camp but it was hard to talk of fun wasn't it? I suppose the other kids went home and talked about camp fires and pillow fights etc., but I remember tears filling up your big beautiful eyes when you looked at Anthony's photos. It was really hard to believe he was dead wasn't it? Then I remember you making Milo, or was it a cuppa tea, for Mum and me, and it tasted just great.

Life just had to go on didn't it? Thank you for sitting with me in church at Anthony's Mass and being so supportive.

You are really a very special nephew to me

Love as always,

Aunty Maureen.

Letter to a brother-in-law

Dearest Jim,

My legs were shaking when I got off the plane and looked for Dad, but there you were striding toward me. Thank you for meeting me at the airport. What could I say and how could I say it? There was no magic wand to wave, and saying Abracadabra wouldn't change a thing. The next few days seemed to be a blur and you must have been physically and emotionally exhausted. When I think back to those two weeks and read my scribbled notes I remember it all so clearly, but now the pain has gone.

The most painful experience shared with you was at the children's hospital. We went together on Thursday morning to see Anthony's body. You were forced to go back to the nursery where Anthony had died and a Sister took us from there to the viewing room. Anthony's body was lying on a white bed and he was covered with a blue blanket. Anthony was dressed in a white cotton jacket with a lace ruffle around the neck, and a white bonnet. Mary had made a posy of two pale pink camellias and jasmine out of her garden. I placed it on Anthony's chest and expected him to open his eyes and say, 'Thanks, the bad dream is over, let's get on with living'. I touched his little cheek and it was cold and then I really understood and accepted that he was dead. Under his bonnet I could see the bruises, obviously where the tubes had been inserted for the transfusion. I remember very clearly the sense of utter loss and bewilderment that engulfed you. We wept together and cuddled each other as we looked at little Anthony on that big bed. We turned to leave and we said 'Thank you' to the Sister. I thought what exemplary manners we had, thanking her for showing us our dead baby, we must be crazy, and I felt like reaching out and hitting her.

We drove back to Mary's in silence. You had to collect Emily and Damien and all the food and flowers that Mary had packed for you to take home. I remember her saying the night before when we had arrived home from the maternity hospital. 'Well the food's started arriving, and ya wanna cuppa tea?' That phrase was to become our joke—every time the doorbell rang we all thought, 'Oh no, another cuppa tea'. I think it helped us all to let off steam and have a laugh. Even though we appreciated the visitors, we joked about how many cups of tea we made over those two weeks.

You collected Carmel from the maternity hospital and I can't begin to imagine how you both felt that morning, going home without a baby. There are a few things I will probably never forget, the first was seeing you and Carmel in her hospital room, surrounded by flowers and cards of congratulations, and I thought to myself Anthony has been and gone. The only flower that I had was a blue forget-me-not out of my Melbourne garden. Carmel showed me the photos taken at the children's hospital, really the only evidence that he had existed. Apparently the official hospital photographer had been to the maternity hospital on Monday morning to take photos but Anthony wouldn't open his eyes, and she would come back later . . . We realised then that it isn't really important if a baby has his eyes open or not.

The other thing I found very difficult was realising that Carmel was still lactating. What a cruel trick nature played, plenty of milk but there was no baby, and there wasn't a switch to turn it off. We will all remember different things about Anthony's death and how they affected us.

Do you remember the kindergarten teacher who said that Emily probably shouldn't go to see Anthony's body? However, you allowed Emily to make her own decision and it was the right one.

Some time later that evening we discussed 'the spirit world'. You had been thinking of your Dad, Aunty Kit and Uncle Gus and our Mum. Would their spirits find Anthony? Who really knows what happens when we die? You reminisced about your Dad and we talked about family history.

I'm glad that I was there to share the tea (and tears) with you.

Lots of love,
Maureen.

Letter to a sister

Dearest Carmel,

My mind is still filled with so many memories of the two weeks I spent with you and Jim after Anthony's death. From the time Jim met me at the airport until I arrived back in Melbourne, it was like a painful slow journey through two weeks. I don't think I will ever forget your face when I saw you lying in your hospital bed; it was as if someone had played a terrible joke on you and you were waiting for them to come and say that the joke was over.

Mary and I rang you the next morning at 8.30 and you were in so much physical pain and of course you were crying and you said 'If only he had been stillborn or sick when he was born it would have been easier.' God knows how much you must have been hurting inside and I felt so useless and helpless.

Mary was worried about Jim's mother and we went to see her to explain what had happened. All she could say over and over was 'Poor Carmel, to think that she carried that baby for nine months. What a shame, poor little baby. I saw him on Sunday and he was so beautiful'. I felt so sad for her as she was all alone and we all had each other.

The worst day of your life must have been when you went home to your empty house.

The discussion with the funeral director seemed so calm as if you and Jim were robots, until he asked for the clothes. It was as if something inside you snapped. You were trying desperately to find a white dress that belonged to Gerard and you said it was his christening dress. All I could think of was that Gerard was still alive and that one day he might want his christening dress for his own children. Would be it fair to give it to Anthony? It seemed to take forever sorting through boxes, cases and drawers. Then you threw yourself on the bed and screamed 'This is barbaric' and so it was. 'Tell me it is not happening to me, please' . . . but it was.

For me I think it was the worst experience of my life seeing you hurting so much and there was nothing I could do to ease the pain. Amidst all the tears and sobs we found a dress, singlet and a nappy and for some reason you were determined to find two nappy pins. I'm not sure why but eventually you decided one would be enough. You held up a bonnet and said 'Will this fit him?' Why weren't we finding clothes to bring him home in? You didn't see him in those clothes, but he really did look beautiful.

One night as I was hanging out the washing you were standing talking to me. As you spoke you were breaking twigs into tiny little pieces and throwing them away. You were angry because you thought Jim was morbid. We had been to see Anthony's body at the chapel that night and you were worried about Jim. I tried to explain that you were both going on the same journey to the same destination but that you would arrive at different times. Everyone grieves differently and he wouldn't think the same as you but that was OK. He had to do it his own way, and we must allow him to take his own time. Then you spoke of the twins in the maternity hospital, and you asked me 'Why wasn't it one of them instead of Anthony'? There was no answer, but you thought that maybe you were stronger than their mother. All I know is that I don't know how I would have coped in the same situation as you.

Emily and Damien both had colds and when you were giving them their medicine, I thought, 'You have to keep going, push on, another minute, hour, day. Keep going for the family who are part of your life.' The shock numbs the brain and it seemed that you functioned like a robot ... do this, do that, cry, crack up, break down, recover and start the whole cycle over again.

Dad came up for lunch on Friday, and he made all the sandwiches. We talked about our childhood. Dad talked about you and how much like Mum you are (your mannerisms etc.). I suppose he was thinking of how terrible it was when Mum died, as he spoke of us kids when we were little. He doesn't reminisce much but he did that day.

You had many visitors, cards, letters and phone calls. Do you remember your ex-neighbour ringing? She said 'Are you still there?' And then you had to tell her that Anthony had been born and died. And so many times after that happened, people at kindergarten etc., who didn't know. But most of all I think of the beautiful flowers that really did fill the house. We both changed our mind about flowers didn't we? It is much better to send them to the house than to the grave as a wreath.

The days seemed to go by in a daze, but we managed. I think Gerard, Emily and Damien kept us on our toes.

I have planned to write these thoughts down for so long but it has been very difficult and as you can see I haven't typed for a long time. However, I decided that I would give this story to you and Jim on Anthony's first birthday. Now I am not so sure that it is a good idea as you are pregnant again, but if you decide to read it I hope that it won't be too painful. And of course you are so much in my thoughts and prayers that this pregnancy will be successful and I look forward to another healthy niece or nephew. Wishing you a healthy and happy pregnancy, Good Luck and lots of love,

Maureen.

Chapter 10

The next pregnancy

*Belief is a child
Who grows up
Into something more than he was.*

*Growing?
What does growing mean?*

*It means a move
In the direction
Of something greater
Than we are at present.*

Ainslie Meares

There is no doubt that the pregnancy following the loss of a baby is an anxious time. When a woman loses a baby she often wishes to become pregnant as soon as possible. However, it does seem important to wait a while as it usually takes a full year or two to recover from the death of a baby. This period of grieving is truly a recuperative one, when the mother has the time to heal her wounded self. When a woman becomes pregnant straight away, she has to deal with both the unresolved grief and her own emotions about the present pregnancy and baby. This can feel like emotional overload and it may also produce a sensation of being torn in two by grief for the baby who has died and joy and anticipation over the future baby.

During the subsequent pregnancy grief may seem to be put to one side so that the woman can focus only on the new baby. If a woman conceives soon after her baby's death, the grief may only be inhibited and may return with greater intensity at the birth of the next baby. This can be most distressing and confusing for the mother. She may wonder which baby she will really be holding and the bonding with the new baby may be placed in jeopardy. In addition, the demands of mothering a new baby require considerable emotional strength. If a lot of the mother's energy is still being used to deal with her grief it can cause her to be less emotionally attuned to her baby. A woman usually knows intuitively when she has emerged from the depth of her grief. Feelings of renewed strength and an ability to focus on the future more than the past often indicate to her that she is ready to become pregnant again.

Although it does seem much easier for those women who have given themselves adequate time to resolve their grief between pregnancies, the next pregnancy will usually bring about feelings of anxiety and worry. Having experienced the tragedy of the death of a baby, it is difficult for a woman not to worry that it may all happen again. She may also worry that even talking about something terrible that is preoccupying her mind may actually make it happen. This may make it hard for her to talk about her fears with her husband, family, friends or doctor. Another barrier to the mother voicing her worries is that those close to her, despite being concerned themselves, may be acting most cheerfully and positively, never mentioning the previous death. It is much more important for the woman to know that she is not alone, and that it is natural for her to worry.

It is vital that the woman's family and friends are receptive to her feelings and listen to her concerns. Being aware of her emotions, which may range from great happiness and joy to times of deep sorrow and anxiety, can assist the mother greatly in her pregnancy and future relationship with her child. The mother needs as much support as possible over this most delicate time of her life.

Opening closed doors

This is not a story about the baby girl I had who was born dead, but of the baby girl I have now and the times between. The labour of the girl I named Sky, I am now convinced, will always be as vivid for me as when she and I were going through it. How would I cope with the labour at the end of my next pregnancy and still love the baby that came to me, hopefully arrive? In retrospect I realise that the fears I held came from the fact that I had learned to withstand a tragic birth and that this had wiped out any instincts I had for coping with a normal healthy baby? One learns how to care for and grieve for a dead baby and how to care for loved ones who are also grieving. So, how can a woman then turn around and go on with the normal happiness that a living baby brings to all those around her; happiness on her account as much as anything. One also learns how to insure against more hurt by closing down certain feelings almost unconsciously. Will one be able to open those closed doors again?

There were certainly no answers for me before my next baby was born. I felt that no one had understood that labour and that therefore no one could reassure me. The tendency of people to keep me from all new babies immediately after Sky was born had made me feel that even outsiders felt that I could not cope with living babies. As I write, I can feel the loneliness of that time and corny as it sounds, laugh at myself for not realising that my next baby was to provide the answer to that loneliness, not immediately, not all at once, but gradually, as with all loving. She would not expect me to think I was lucky I had her, even if I did not have my baby Sky. She did not demand great happiness at her birth, when my sadness was overwhelming, because I could not have the both of them. She just needed to be loved, in a most undemanding way.

The fears I had as to whether she would continue to be healthy were not answered convincingly by the doctors.

They had been unable to tell me why Sky had died and yet tried to tell me for sure that my next baby girl would be just fine. I wanted to believe them but could not for sure. The baby herself could tell me nothing; she was there, once again undemanding, filling that loneliness. And so in a way, the baby bonded with me. Not in the way I had expected, not in the way others expected and saw us to be, but in a way which was ours and was plenty.

As time goes on, I realise that my fears of bonding were real and valid fears. I could not say I bonded with her in a way which, before Sky, would have been normal for me and a new baby child. Certainly our relationship is very different from that which I have with my son who is older than Sky, but of course that could have been so in any event. I still worry she will die, I still look at her and say I wish I could love you better, but I now realise that all these things make up our loving.

Appendix:
the professional
overview

How may a member of the
clergy help?

BRIAN HEATH

Because my son of three days old died and because my
daughter of three years old died, and because I have been a
member of the clergy for over thirty years, I believe I have
experiences which might be of some value to recently
bereaved parents.

In one sense, the cause of death is beside the point. The
fact of death and the pain of death are where we are.

Most parents have been conditioned by our Western
culture into believing that life is logical. Then we go on to
believe that death too is logical. We believe that if we can
attach some reason to the death of our child, then that will
act as an antidote and lessen the agony. We are therefore likely
to encounter such pious phrases as 'It was the will of God.'
'He has gone to be with the angels.' 'The Lord gave and the
Lord has taken away.' I hear such phrases as a bit of neat
ecclesiastical footwork, which enables clergy or well-meaning
Christians to sidestep the issue.

I don't believe that the death of either of my children was
'the will of God', nor do I believe that their deaths were due

to 'the Lord taking away'. I know that such comments are a desperate attempt on the part of caring people to lessen the pain of grieving parents, but in the long term they are far more likely to alienate parents from the God who could be a source of comfort and healing.

In the course of my training, I received minimal instruction as to how best to minister to bereaved parents. Life experience, however, has instructed me well. I now know that instead of attempting banal theological explanations, I do better to become again a grieving parent and allow my tears to mingle with theirs or allow my shouts of anger and confusion to add to the volume of their own. 'My God, my God, why hast thou forsaken me!!!' (Not question marks but exclamation marks.)

If you are a grieving parent, I will not preach to you, even though I have an abundant supply of fine-sounding phrases and Biblical texts. Rather, we will touch each other and be silent in our shared pain. And in that silence you will know that I, too, am incensed at the apparent injustice and illogic of your loss. Or, on the other hand, you may regard me as a representative of that God whom you believe to have forsaken you, and you may well wish to rail at me verbally or even physically. I will receive your anger and will not strike back because I have caught a glimpse of the measure of your pain. Even if my eyes were dry, I would be weeping with you because our humanness hangs heavily on us at such a time.

A Jewish rabbi, Harold Kushner, has written a wonderful book called *When bad things happen to good people*. In it he reminds us of our habit of hunting for logic and he begs us to accept the fact of 'randomness' or illogic, in our world. When we are able to do that, we no longer see God as the source of our misfortune. We see Him as one who weeps with us. We begin to recognise Him as a source of healing.

When I was invited to write this chapter, I was delighted, because I have known Margaret Nicol and her work for many years. We have been good friends, sharing tears and laughter, loss and gain, as that randomness touched our respective lives. At the risk of sounding like Pollyanna or seeming to contradict what I said earlier, we have frequently found pain to have a unique transformative quality. Pain is not always like a nuclear blast which destroys all life; it may be compared to a bushfire which ultimately promotes new growth.

Now I want to make some functional comments.

Twenty or thirty years ago, laymen were taught to avoid at all costs allowing a child to die unbaptised. It was believed that tragic consequences would follow. This belief produced high drama in some movies. Unhappily the idea persists for mainy laymen of many different church affiliations. Enlightened thinking and Christian compassion have led us to modify or abandon the notion of a God who allows his love to be shackled by a ceremony or ritual. I acknowledge that there is comfort for parents if their baby can be 'marked' with the traditional Christian symbol and this service can be provided by any Christian person. However, if such a ceremony is not available, there may be 'baptism by desire', where there is no ceremony but the infant is considered baptised by the desire of the parents.

Many parents who experience the death of a young baby may have no direct church affiliations. That may make them reluctant to call upon the services of clergy, particularly at some inconvenient hour. No doubt there are some members of the clergy who would not respond positively to such a need, but the majority would not be concerned about the hour or the 'our'. The most reliable way to find a suitable person is through a local funeral director, who will be in touch with all local clergy and will be able to suggest the most appropriate person.

In some instances parents may have to decide whether or not to allow other siblings to see the baby that has died. There would be a strong tendency to 'protect' them from emotional pain. In many instances, parents might feel guilty about the death of their baby. That sense of guilt would further inhibit them from 'sharing' the death visually with other siblings.

However, it is my firm conviction that such sharing could enable both the parents and siblings, regardless of age, to move through the stages of grief with modified pain.

It may be that parents will want to plan a funeral service that relates intimately to their own needs. On the other hand, parents may choose to leave the service totally to the discretion of the person who will conduct it. For me, there are no rigid rules and I am guided by pastoral more than theological issues.

In one instance parents chose to have their baby at home for a number of days before the funeral service. He was dressed in his usual clothing and surrounded by his best-loved toys. Other parents might find such contact with their dead baby more than they could bear.

If parents decide to plan a funeral service themselves, they could receive assistance from a member of the clergy. It would be reasonable to use readings from the Bible but there is no reason why appropriate readings from secular literature should not also be used. It may be that a friend or relative would read at the service. The same is true of prayers. They could be prepared beforehand, or they could be prayed without preparation by the clergy or by a layman. It might be that parents would like to use specific music which is meaningful for them. The parents might determine that they alone will be present at this final contact with their baby. On the other hand, they may choose to share this moment of their grief with family and friends. In all such preparation, the primary issue is to meet the needs of the parents as fully as possible. Hopefully, they will be in touch with a member of the clergy who is sensitive in this area of grief. That is not inevitable and should they feel that their needs are not being met, or that their wishes are being overruled, they are fully entitled to ask to be in touch with someone else.

One of the issues which parents will have to resolve is whether to bury or cremate their baby. Apart from any religious factors, the difference in cost is considerable. In many places, the cost for burial is up to four times that for cremation. Some parents may not need to consider that aspect, but there would be many who would be adding to their discomfort by having an unnecessary financial burden. Unfortunately, bereaved parents are very susceptible. They might easily be persuaded that they 'owe it' to their baby to choose burial, simply because it is more expensive.

For most parents who suffer the death of a young baby, the shock is intense. Under such circumstances, it is extremely difficult to make well-balanced decisions. A member of the clergy may be able to assist in this regard by presenting parents with the advantages and disadvantages of various options. In the case of cremation, some Cemetery Boards are prepared to safeguard the ashes for up to six months in order to give the parents time to make an appropriate decision.

A funeral service or a cremation service may vary enormously in the time they take. They vary also in their form. There are further variations which depend on the denomination of the clergy. It would be impossible to define each possibility.

The member of the clergy may be invited to the home after the funeral service, which I recognise has its value, and such an invitation would normally be accepted. Ideally, the member of the clergy would maintain contact with the family. If they are part of his parish, that happens automatically. However, 80% of the services I conduct are for people outside the parish and continuing contact is very difficult. Clearly that creates a dilemma for me. I choose, therefore, to remind family and friends that support is usually needed for a long time after the last bouquet of flowers has died.

A paediatrician's view of neonatal death

DR. J. R. TOMPKINS M.B., B.S., F.R.A.C.P.
Department of Newborn Services
King Edward Memorial Hospital for Women

Doctors working with newborn babies are never far from the issues of life and death. Much of their work is with mothers and babies where the possibility of some risk of abnormality was anticipated, but either did not eventuate or was easily overcome, and they are then able to share with satisfaction the joy of the parents in their new baby. But there are many other occasions when serious problems arise and where there are real threats to the baby's survival.

Optimally, the care of a sick baby will have started prior to birth. Where there has been warning of the impending birth of a baby likely to have problems, the obstetrician and neonatalogist would have had time to consult with each other and to discuss possible events and outcomes with the anxious parents. Some of the anxiety of the parents can thus be directed towards real possibilities, and they can be reassured where reassurance is appropriate. Often though, babies arrive too quickly for prior discussion to have taken place, or where the mother has been too ill to be fully aware, or when the father is away. It is then particularly that the health professionals dealing with the baby and family must be aware of and sensitive to the special concerns and needs of the parents.

Neonatal care has reached the stage where nearly every bodily function can be monitored or measured, and supported if necessary. Often the baby seems overwhelmed by the tubes, wires, screens and sounds. Amidst all of this, the parents need to be helped to see beyond the technology and to relate to their baby. They will do this directly, by touching and holding, and talking to their baby, and also indirectly and symbolically by giving a name, by taking photographs, by providing articles of clothing and small toys.

The bond between parents and their babies is well recognised, but it can be easily forgotten that this bond has grown throughout the pregnancy. Parents often think ahead of the baby, to the child, even the adult, that will result from pregnancy. Parents will have anticipated the changes in their lives with the responsibilities that their new family member will bring. When a baby is in danger, it is not just the dream that parents have for their baby's life which is threatened, but the dream of their own fulfilled lives.

When a baby is sick, the parents often find themselves struggling with confusing and conflicting thoughts and emotions. Their first fear is that their baby might die, or might manage to survive with some unbearable problem. It can be hard for them to reach a realistic assessment of the situation. Their mood can fluctuate from optimism to gloom with each minor change in their baby's condition. It may be impossible for them to believe the advice they have been given, and they may worry unnecessarily about trivial problems, or hold on to hope beyond the end of hope.

At the same time, the staff may be confronting a variety of issues outside those immediately affecting the baby's medical and nursing care. Very difficult assessments may need to be made of the baby's prospects for survival with or without permanent damage or handicap. If it seems to the parents and everyone involved with their baby that further intensive care measures are likely to be futile, a decision may be made to cease the life support which has by then become inappropriate. When these hard decisions are finally made, the parents' great sadness can be touched with relief as they can then be with their baby in a quiet room, away from the intrusive activity of intensive care.

The initial reaction of parents to a baby who has died may be one of not wanting to see the baby. This may be because they think they might not be able to cope with their feelings. We know now that to see and hold their dead baby is an emotional and important experience for parents, which can help them eventually come to terms with the reality of their baby's life and death. It is vital to help parents to take this step, as it is almost unknown for parents later to regret this contact with their baby; parents who miss this opportunity sometimes later wish that they had seen their baby. The staff can help to preserve memories of the baby by offering the parents photographs, footprints, a lock of hair; if parents are not ready to accept these, they should be carefully kept in the baby's file.

Intensive care staff focus their attention on the needs of the baby but try also to meet the parents' needs. This can be difficult for the staff members, who must combine clinical care and decision-making with an understanding and feeling for the emotions, the hopes and the fears of the parents. Given the nature of neonatal intensive care units and the fluctuating workload, it is inevitable that there may be some times when parents feel pushed into the background. Intensive care units are very stressful for staff as well as parents, and people working under stress may find themselves without the time or the emotional capacity to reach beyond the baby's immediate needs to those of the family. This is when support for parents from other family members and friends, and from other health professionals not immediately involved in the care of the baby, is so beneficial.

Amongst those who care for newborn babies there is no longer ignorance of the needs of grieving parents. We must strive to meet these needs by providing both the facilities and the staff with appropriate skills. In the wider community, the silence which has long surrounded the topic of perinatal death is at last being broken. In her research, Margaret Nicol has given us the information that we must now use, to bring comfort to those parents whose loss can be so hard to bear.

An obstetrician's view of stillbirth, neonatal death and other reproductive loss

ASSOCIATE PROFESSOR P. F. H. GILES
M.Sc., M.B., Ch.B., F.R.C.O.G., F.R.A.C.O.G.
Department of Obstetrics and Gynaecology
The University of Western Australia

Soon after I joined the Department of Obstetrics and Gynaecology in the University of Western Australia in 1966 I realised that I knew little about the reactions of mothers whose babies had been born dead, or had died some days after birth. In 1968 and 1969, because I could find nothing about this subject in current textbooks or medical journals, I studied the reactions of 40 women who had lost babies. I did this in the hope of gaining an insight into how they had been affected and how they could be helped. It has been heartening to see the ever-increasing interest in this problem in recent years.

The way in which mothers, fathers, other children, nurses and doctors react to such deaths, and how we can help those so bereaved, is discussed below.

What are mothers' reactions to the loss of a baby?

These reactions were not described by doctors until 1970 when three research papers appeared. They came from Kennell's team in Cleveland, Ohio; from Wolff and his team at the University of Illinois and from myself in Perth, Western Australia. The principal findings of those studies were:

Mothers wanted to hear of their babies, deaths when they occurred and not at a time that was thought perhaps to be more appropriate by medical or nursing staff. Each mother showed the classical features of the grief reaction: emptiness, sadness, restlessness, numbness, tiredness, self-blame, and questioning repeatedly why her baby had died. Many mothers also felt that they had failed their husbands or that they would never have a live baby.

Many experienced shock and disbelief at their babies' death. Most had no warning during the pregnancy that their babies might die.

These reactions occurred irrespective of whether the babies had lived a week or only an hour, or had weighed 3000 grams or only 500 grams.

Many parents were not prepared for their own mourning responses and the mother's and father's differing reactions commonly disturbed their relationship.

The next milestone in the study of the reactions of mothers to the death of their babies in the perinatal period was by Emanuel Lewis of London in 1976. He drew attention to the special problems of the mother of a stillborn baby. He made the observation that because society abhors a stillbirth it is not surprising that a mother may feel that she is avoided by her doctor, her partner and her friends. The mother, too, tended to withdraw, to isolate herself, because of her own feelings of failure.

In 1982, at King Edward Memorial Hospital, Perth, Western Australia, Margaret Nicol and Jeff Tompkins studied 110 women at 6 to 36 months after they had lost babies as stillbirths or neonatal deaths. These researchers found that 21% of these mothers showed a marked measurable deterioration in physical health. Their other important finding was that the 21% above could be easily identified because:

- they had had a crisis during the pregnancy
- or they did not consider that their partners or family were supportive
- or they had seen but had not held their dead baby.

The above results suggest that it was these women who should be given additional support by hospital staff with a view to preventing a prolonged or severe grief reaction. What made this research so potentially useful was the fact that it was found to be easy to identify the women most at risk of a severe grief reaction.

The last research findings I would like to mention are those of Wilson's team in South Dakota. In 1982 they studied eight families who had lost both newborn twins, and eight families who had lost only one of the twins. The study found that presence of one live twin did not lessen the grieving process. Friends and hospital staff, however, tended to assume that the grief would be lessened by the presence of a surviving twin. Thus they saw no need, or less need, to support such families nor to offer parents the opportunity to mourn the twin who had died.

The father's reaction to perinatal death

Common reactions of fathers to perinatal death are self-blame, anger and a feeling of helplessness in knowing how to support their partners.

In many cases the father's grief seems to be less intense and less prolonged than that of the mother. This apparent difference of grieving has been found to stress the relationship. One investigator found that about one in three marriages developed serious difficulties after a perinatal death. Warning parents of these problems and encouraging them to share their feelings might help to avoid this additional setback to the family.

The reactions of other children

If the mother and father are depressed, preoccupied or irritable after the death of their new baby, the other children may feel abandoned and unloved.

Well-meant explanations given to children ('your baby brother has been taken by God', '. . . or is asleep') may give them distorted ideas about doctors, illness and death.

The other children need to grieve, to have their questions answered and to feel loved. A simple truthful explanation 'Mummy and Daddy are sad, our new baby was too small to live') may help the other children to grasp that death is irreversible, inevitable and natural, and that it is no one's fault. The children should also be reassured that healthy children do not die suddenly.

One of the difficulties in this area is that the very parents who are enmeshed in their own grief are those less likely to recognise that their other children also need help.

Doctors and the bereaved mothers

I found in my study that doctors readily prescribed sedatives for bereaved mothers and treated physical symptoms conscientiously, but that they avoided discussing the baby's death with the mother. This was put down to their probable inability to provide support for others when they them- selves were feeling defeated by, or perhaps in some way responsible for, the death. Doctors do feel shocked by the death and must resolve their feelings of failure, guilt, helpless- ness and anger before they are able to support the parents.

Other studies show that a stillbirth caused a deterioration in the doctor–patient relationship; doctors tended to avoid such mothers and to discharge them early from hospital.

Dr. Wendy Savage, of London, records how helpless and useless she felt at the first stillbirth she attended. She also describes the accompanying awful feeling of emptiness and of numbed horror. Other reactions seen in the attending doctor include denial (checking and re-checking for foetal heart sounds), anger directed at others concerned with the patient's care, shame and guilt. Some doctors become overcautious, tending to order many tests and to do more Caesarean sections.

One of the major causes of job dissatisfaction amongst doctors who specialise in looking after newborn babies arises from their having to deal with angry or disappointed parents.

Not every baby will be born alive and healthy. Deaths still occur. Most are unavoidable.

Education of pregnant women about stillbirth and neonatal death

The Royal College of Obstetricians and Gynaecologists recently highlighted the fact that little or no reference was made to obstetric disasters in many of the booklets published to help women prepare for childbirth. The emphasis on health and normality tended to reduce parents' awareness of the possibility of miscarriage, stillbirth or neonatal death. Miscarriages occur quite frequently, in 15–20% of all pregnancies, and many occur because the foetus has not developed normally. Parents should be aware that there is usually nothing wrong with either of them when this happens. However, three or four successive miscarriages occurring at about the same stage of pregnancy do call for expert advice.

Parents should be aware that even these days there is a small but definite risk of stillbirth or neonatal death of the baby. The College recommends that antenatal booklets and leaflets should draw attention to that fact, give advice on how it is managed and on how bereaved parents might be helped.

The nurse and prenatal death

The nurse, like the doctor, must recognise and resolve his or her own feelings of failure, guilt, helplessness and anger, which result from the death, before he or she can help the bereaved parents.

The mother wants from the nurse sympathy and empathy rather than scientific reasons for the baby's death. The nurse can provide such support:
- by sitting beside and listening to the mother
- by avoiding platitudes, and especially by avoiding pious platitudes ('It's God's will', 'Time will heal')

- by respecting the way that the mother and father express their grief
- by being willing to talk about the baby and by calling the baby by name if one has been given
- by demonstrating that he or she does care.

Nurses should be prepared in their training for the stress that perinatal death may cause in themselves and in their colleagues. Care and support should be available for nurses too.

Grief and the importance of mourning

When I was a medical student and young doctor I received no instruction on grief nor on the importance of mourning. In fact, much of the work in this field was done after I had graduated.

Freud, as long ago as 1917, pointed out that grief is not abnormal. It is the self-limited reaction to the loss of a beloved person.

Later studies, especially those of Lindemann (1944), showed that grief had psychological and physical features—numbness, disbelief, sadness, a feeling of emptiness in the upper abdomen, loss of appetite. Grief has three phases which merge with one another. Initially there is a stage of shock lasting up to 14 days which is characterised by crying, emptiness and numbness. This is followed by a stage, lasting up to six months, characterised by preoccupation with the deceased. Finally, there is a stage of resolution.

Parkes (1975) drew attention to the fact that grief affects both mental and physical health. Following the death of a husband or wife there is an increased death rate (due mainly to heart disease) and an increase in admissions to psychiatric hospitals (because of depression).

An important contribution came from Maddison and Walker (1967). They showed that inadequate mourning and suppression of grief hindered psychological recovery.

Is grief after the loss of a baby comparable with the grief experienced after the death of an older person?

Helene Deutsch (1945) maintained that grief after perinatal death was not the same as grief following the death of an adult relative. She felt that it was rather the nonfulfilment of a wish fantasy, grieving for the potential that could now never be realised.

Peppers and Knapp (1980) measured mothers' grief responses to miscarriage, stillbirth and neonatal death. The grief scores were found to be quite similar in each of those losses. They concluded that affectional ties developed very early in pregnancy.

Furman (1978) has a different view. He feels that the foetus is not regarded by the mother as a separate person but as a part of the mother's body, and that this continues for some time after birth. He considers that the mother's reaction to loss of her baby was akin to her probable reaction to the loss of a limb. She needs time to readjust to herself as an incomplete human being. During that readjustment she will feel empty, depressed and lack self-esteem.

In my experience, each of these three views has something to commend it.

Mourning a stillborn baby

If parents have not seen their stillborn baby they may have no actual person to mourn. Because memories facilitate mourning, and because mourning is important, then it would seem most important that parents should see, hold and touch their dead baby so that they will have memories to help the mourning process.

Giving the baby a name, taking a photograph, holding a funeral, are other activities which should aid mourning, provided that they conform with the cultural and religious tenets of the parents.

Loss of a baby

Grief that follows adoption

Condon (1986) reported in the *Medical Journal of Australia* that many mothers who had had their babies adopted, subsequently had long-standing unresolved grief reactions. This is not surprising in the light of our knowledge of the mourning process and of the importance of memories. Many of the mothers felt that their children were 'missing', or had fantasies that they were ill or unhappy. They had no clear idea of what they had given up, as many had not seen or held their children.

Condon suggested that a mother relinquishing her baby should be encouraged to hold and breast-feed her baby, and be offered a photograph.

How the doctor can help the parents

In my original article on this subject in the *Australian and New Zealand Journal of Obstetrics and Gynaecology* (1970) I wrote:

> Telling the mother about her child's death should not be delayed. It should be done sympathetically and factually by the doctor himself, preferably in a quiet place where she will have no inhibitions about breaking down. Initially, she and her husband may be too stunned to take in anything but the fact that the child has died. Later a simple, rational explanation of the cause of death will relieve fear, misconception and guilt. Such matters as being in a single room, seeing or not seeing the baby, sedation, and early discharge, can be discussed. What she prefers will depend on her cultural, religious and social background. Allowing her to talk and answering her repeated questions patiently will help her, as will reassuring her that nothing she did (or failed to do) caused the death and that her feelings of sadness, restless- ness, exhaustion or failure are understandable. Any hostility she shows may be part of her reaction to the loss and should not blindly be interpreted as personal resentment. 'A willing ear, tolerant of confusion and anger ... is probably more important than tonics or sedatives.'

When the post-mortem report and results of any special investigations are available, the prognosis for a future pregnancy should be discussed factually. The patient should be left in no doubt as to when she may start another pregnancy if she wishes.

Women with intra-uterine death of more than a few days duration were not seen in the present series. On the principles already considered it would seem advisable that the doctor tell the patient the diagnosis as soon as it is made, reassure her that nothing she has done has caused it and that its presence will do her no harm, and let her know clearly and simply what management is planned.

To have relieved a patient's anxiety, loneliness and guilt, and to have established her trust and confidence for the future are the rewards of a doctor's readiness to talk with a woman who has lost her baby in the prenatal period.

Over the years I have found little more to add to that advice. I cannot overemphasise the importance of listening patiently. I am sure that it is important to help create memories of the dead child. It is also important to let parents know what reactions are likely, and to reassure them that anger, sleeplessness, sadness and restlessness are normal reactions to their loss. Some parents may feel no particular reactions; others may feel that they are going mad. Both are normal reactions. As this can be a time of stress between mother and father, they should be warned of that and that the needs of other children should not be overlooked.

The thought of a post-mortem examination on their dead baby may upset parents. In my opinion a post-mortem examination should be done on all babies born dead or dying in the perinatal period. Three years after I had graduated as a doctor, I returned to the Department of Pathology at the University of Otago Medical School. The first post-mortem I performed was on a stillborn baby. The obstetrician was concerned because the death had been quite unexpected. Post-mortem examination showed that the baby had no kidneys. This allowed me to reassure the obstetrician that nothing he did (or did not do) was responsible for the baby's death, and he in turn was able to tell the parents exactly what had caused the death of their baby and to explain to them the risk of such a condition occurring in another pregnancy. Sometimes a post-mortem does not show why a baby died, but the finding that there were no congenital defects can be reassuring to parents in further pregnancies.

How long after a stillbirth or a neonatal death should a woman wait until she tries to conceive again? In my opinion she should wait until she has completed her grieving for her dead child, and that may be anything from six to twelve months, or longer. Many older women or women who have had trouble conceiving understandably prefer not to wait that long.

Other reproductive loss and its effects

Infertility: Irreversible losses can be dealt with, but there is no resolution of grief when there is grief plus hope, as commonly occurs in infertile women. Resolution of such grief may be all the more difficult when there is little support from friends and family. By being willing listeners we can show that we do care, and help the depression, anger and grief commonly felt by the infertile.

Miscarriage: Only recently have the psychological effects of a miscarriage ('spontaneous abortion' in medical terminology) been recognised. It is a time of loss, grieving is common, but this is not generally acknowledged by friends, family or caregivers. When given permission to express their feelings, these women reveal their anger, bitterness, sense of failure and sadness. Many women who miscarry may feel that they are somehow personally responsible or that they will not be able to carry a live child.

Termination of a pregnancy for foetal malformation: Whilst there seems to be little reaction to termination of an early pregnancy performed at a woman's request, there is a marked and commonly prolonged grief reaction when pregnancy is terminated because of a foetal malformation. In most of these cases it is the loss of a baby *wanted* by the parents. Caregivers and friends may find it difficult to offer sympathy in such cases; they tend to view the loss of a malformed baby as a blessing in disguise.

Hospital services for the bereaved

Perinatal bereavement clinics have been established in some obstetrical hospitals. In addition to providing organised support for parents they have an important educative function and can influence for the better the way the needs of the bereaved are met in the hospital.

Booklets on perinatal death likewise can provide information not only for bereaved parents but for nurses, medical students, doctors, other caregivers and the community at large. Several excellent booklets have been produced by the self-help group SANDS (Stillbirth and Neonatal Death Support).

Much more can be done to educate hospital staff in caring for bereaved parents. Discussion groups may make them more aware of their own reactions and of the reactions of their colleagues. Attendance at meetings of self-help support groups may make them really aware of the reactions of parents and of the deficiencies of care in hospital.

Conclusion

Until the 1970's the need to support and rehabilitate a family in which there had been a stillbirth or neonatal death was not widely recognised. Since that time we have become increasingly aware of the reactions such a loss can cause in the mother, the father, the other children, and the various caregivers. Studies on grief and the importance of mourning have made us more aware of how we may effectively help the bereaved.

References

Condon, J. T., 1986. Psychological disability in women who relinquish a baby for adoption. *The Medical Journal of Australia* 144: 119.

Deutsch, H., 1945. *The Psychology of Women: a psycho-analytic interpretation*, Vol. 2, *Motherhood*, p.263. Grune & Stratton, New York.

Freud, S., 1917. *Mourning and Melancholia*. Standard Edition, Hogarth Press, London, 14: 243–258.

Furman, E. P., 1978. The death of a newborn: care of the parents. *Birth and the Family Journal*, 5: 214–218.

Giles, P. F. H., 1970. Reactions of women to perinatal death. *Australian and New Zealand Journal of Obstetrics & Gynaecology*, 10: 207–210.

Kennell, J. H., Slyter, H., Klaus, M. H., 1970. The mourning response of parents to the death of a newborn infant. *New England Journal of Medicine*, 283: 344–349.

Lewis, E., 1976. The management of stillbirth: coping with an unreality. *Lancet* ii: 619–620.

Lewis, E., 1979. Mourning by the family after a stillbirth or neonatal death. *Archives of Disease in Childhood*, 54, 303–306.

Lindemann, E., 1944. Symptomatology and management of acute grief. *American Journal of Psychiatry*, 101: 141–148.

Maddison, D., Walker, W. L., 1967. Factors affecting the outcome of conjugal bereavement. *British Journal of Psychiatry* 113: 1057–1067.

Nicol, M. T., Tompkins, J. R., Campbell, N. A., 1982a. Mothers' views of perinatal death: implications for care. *Australian Paediatric Journal* 18: 141.

Nicol, M. T., Tompkins, J. R., Campbell, N. A. 1982b. Maternal bereavement: factors affecting mothers' responses to perinatal death. *Australian Paediatric Journal* 18: 142.

Parkes, C. M., 1975. The broken heart. In: *Bereavement*, Ch. 2, pp. 29–45. Penguin Books, Middlesex.

Peppers, L. G., Knapp, R. J., 1980. Maternal reactions to involuntary fetal/infant death. *Psychiatry* 43: 155–159.

Savage, W., 1978. Perinatal loss and the medical team. *Midwife, Health Visitor and Community Nurse*. Part 1, 14: 292–295, Part 2, 14: 348–351.

Wilson, A. L., Fenton, L. J., Stevens, D. C., Soule, D. J.1982. The death of a newborn twin: an analysis of parental bereavement. Paediatrics 70: 587-591.

Wolff, J. R., Nielson, P. E., Schiller, P., 1970. The emotional reaction to a stillbirth. *American Journal of Obstetrics & Gynaecology* 108: 73–77.